Yoga for Scuba Divers

By Kimberlee Jensen Stedl and Todd Stedl, Ph.D.

Published by 8th Element Yoga, a division of
8th Element Recreation LLC
1916 Pike Place
Suite 12-440
Seattle, WA 98101

Published in Seattle, Washington, USA.

Printed in the United States of America.

First edition: July 2007

ISBN 978-0-6151-5432-9

Visit us on the Web at

www.8thElementYoga.com
and
www.8thElementDiving.com

For everyone working to keep our oceans vibrant.

Acknowledgements

We would like to acknowledge our friends at Blue Frontier Diving and Pelagia Scuba, along with our diving buddies, for all their support and for their participation in our workshops.

We would like to thank Planet Earth Yoga, for being a great yoga studio for hosting our workshops in Seattle. We also would like to thank all of the students who attended our workshops. We have enjoyed learning from you as much as we enjoyed teaching you.

Todd would like to thank Perry and LaDonna Tamarra, Truxton and Lavonne Terkla, Josh Meramore, Mischi Carter, Terry Miller, and Craig Gillespie for being great role models as dive instructors.

Kimberlee would like to thank all of her yoga teachers and teacher-trainers who have taught her. She would particularly like to thank Joanne Hill of Seattle, WA for making her yoga classes tremendous fun and Stephanie Adams of Hood River, OR for being a great yoga instructor role model.

We would like to thank Elizabeth Worcester and Jeff Simpson for the photo of us at our wedding that we used in the About the Authors section.

Finally, we would like to thank our families for encouraging us to swim and to enjoy the water as children, which has stayed with us throughout our lives. Thanks also for supporting us in all our crazy escapades.

Table of Contents

Disclaimer

This book is for self-knowledge and is not a substitute for consulting with a physician or physical therapist. Please consult your physician before beginning a new physical conditioning program, especially if you have a pre-existing condition for which you are being treated or you have been inactive for a long period of time. All the poses in this book assume the reader is physically capable of these poses; however, they do carry risks and only you and your health care providers can say what poses work and do not work for your body at this point in time.

Women who are pregnant must consult with their physician before practicing yoga poses and are advised to take a pre-natal yoga class instead of doing a general yoga practice. Pregnant women are also strongly advised not to scuba dive.

People recovering from injuries should consult with their doctor or their physical therapist as certain poses may aggravate an injury and delay healing. We strongly advise taking this book with you to your physicians and asking them to select the appropriate poses for you, especially if you see a physician or take medication regularly for a known condition, or if you have previously suffered from decompression sickness (DCS—"the bends").

None of the poses in this book should be performed while wearing scuba gear. All of the poses are intended to be performed on land, not under water. Performing yoga under water eliminates the strength benefits of the poses because of the weightless environment, and dealing with buoyancy issues while trying to perform some poses under water can be strenuous, which increases the risk of getting DCS.

Strenuous exercise before or after scuba diving has also been linked to an increased risk of getting DCS. This is especially true if a diver has previously suffered from DCS. All of the poses in this book can be performed non-strenuously, assuming the reader is physically capable of these poses. As an extra measure of caution, we recommend buffering your dives with a few minutes of quiet time on each end: do some pre-dive warm-up poses, get geared up, and then spend a few minutes visualizing a smooth dive before entering the water; immediately after the dive, spend a few minutes meditating about your underwater experience, and then finish with some post-dive recovery poses after stowing your dive gear.

Basketball is an endurance sport, and you have to learn to control your breath. That's the essence of yoga, too. So I consciously began to use yoga techniques in my practice and playing.

—Kareem Abdul-Jabbar

Introduction

When we first met, Todd had just fallen in love with scuba diving and Kimberlee was beginning her yoga teacher-training program. Todd managed to convince Kimberlee to jump into the waters of Puget Sound, which rarely heat up past 50° Fahrenheit. In exchange, Todd agreed to turn himself upside down and twist like a pretzel. As we exchanged knowledge, we discovered the synchronicity of yoga and scuba diving, such as the emphasis on breath. In both yoga and scuba diving classes, instructors tell students that if they remember just one thing, they must remember to keep breathing.

The more Todd learned various yoga poses and developed his personal practice, the more comfortable and efficient he felt under water with both his breathing and his movement. As we began to construct our workshops, Kimberlee analyzed the mechanics of scuba diving and developed a functional fitness program for divers based on yoga poses. Since we both personally had wonderful experiences with meditation techniques, we incorporated guided meditation and visualizations into our workshops. Finally, as we contemplated writing *Yoga for Scuba Divers*, we realized how yoga principles coincided with conservation movements in scuba diving. For example, the more divers that practice principles such as non-greed, the more we can preserve the reefs for all divers to enjoy.

We hope you benefit from both the physical practices and the philosophical practices we introduce you to in this book. *Yoga for Scuba Divers* is not a comprehensive resource on everything yoga has to offer, and we encourage you to continue your studies if yoga has peaked your interest. *Yoga for Scuba Divers* is, however, a wonderful introduction to yoga that can enhance your experience as a scuba diver.

What is yoga?

Yoga is one of six systems of ancient Indian philosophy dating back more than 5,000 years. Even though many people consider yoga merely a stretching and breathing exercise, it goes far beyond that. Yoga itself is a mental and philosophical practice. Yoga is not a religion and does not prescribe a belief system to you, but through the meditative aspect of yoga, you can develop a greater connection with your own spirituality. The term *yoga* in Sanskrit means to yoke, or to unify. Through this practice you unite the body and the mind, which in the West we have often separated. You also unite yourself with your belief system, whatever it may be.

There are several braches of yoga. Most often in the West you will encounter royal *(raja)* yoga, also known as active yoga. This form of yoga is organized into eight components, called limbs. The first seven limbs are considered steps on the way to the final limb, liberation *(samadhi)*. When people hear the word yoga, though, they generally think of only the third limb of royal yoga, which deals with poses *(asanas)*. Scores of books devoted to the poses fill bookshops, but ironically, in the foundational text for royal yoga the only thing ever written about the poses is this: "*Asana* is a steady, comfortable seat."

How we got from that comfortable seat to wrapping our ankles around our neck is quite a journey. Along the way, yogis realized our bodies needed training in order to sit and meditate for long periods of time, so they developed various pose exercises to work the kinks out so yogis could sit still. Many believed that for us to quiet the mind in meditation, we must first exhaust the body. Another theory we have is that ancient yogis created lots of complex and intricate poses by looking for new ways to challenge themselves and thus created some rather acrobatic poses. Over the years, many yoga teachers have codified and developed various sequences based on principles of the body and the goal of balancing the various major muscle groups of the body. By the end of the 20th century, medical researchers and physical therapists had influenced yoga practices by adding Western medicine's knowledge of the musculoskeletal system to yoga pose practices. In turn, many physicians began recommending yoga to their patients for medical concerns such as stress relief, back pain, insomnia and depression.

How can yoga help scuba diving?

The foundation of most yoga classes is breath work, which is loosely based on one of the limbs of yoga called *prana*, or life force. Many yoga teachers view the yoga poses as simply a means to enhance your breathing. Likewise, the primary rule in scuba diving is to keep breathing. The rhythmic breathing techniques used in yoga will help you keep your breath slow and steady throughout a dive. By breathing this way while diving you stay relaxed, which enables you to make better decisions under water.

In addition to the breath work, yoga poses help scuba divers develop the strength and muscle endurance required for diving. When you dive you use muscles that many of us don't often use on land, but specific yoga poses can target and strengthen those muscle groups before you hit the water. Yoga poses also enhance balance and flexibility, which helps prevent injury and gives you better control in the weightless environment under water. Also, when you dive you have a limited range of motion; we have all learned to keep our arms still and to use small controlled strokes while finning. However, the cartilage in our joints receives no blood supply and relies upon synovial fluid for nutrients. Joints receive adequate synovial fluid distribution only when you move them through their full range of motion. By performing various poses in yoga you will move almost all of your joints through their full range of motion, keeping your joints well nourished and healthy.

Unlike many forms of exercise where the body does one thing while the mind does another—such as riding a stationary bicycle while reading a magazine—yoga integrates the two by asking you to mind your alignment and your breath in the pose. By using this same physical awareness in your home yoga practice, you will fine-tune your internal sensors. This development of focus and awareness translates directly to scuba diving, because it will help make you more aware of your breathing, your temperature, and even your surroundings. More awareness makes you a safer diver.

In this book, we will teach you key poses for divers, some basic anatomy, and breath exercises for your physical practice. Also, we introduce visualization and meditation techniques to prepare you psychologically for diving. Finally, we discuss a few yoga lifestyle guidelines that directly correlate to diver ethics. Enjoy the journey.

The importance of breath

Breathing is unique in that it's the only bodily function that is both involuntary and voluntary. Our bodies keep breathing without any conscious effort, but yet we can consciously control our respiration. We can't do that with the beating of our heart, so our respiratory system is really unlike other systems.

Relaxed, full, steady breathing is essential to yoga, and yogis have invented several breathing exercises to master the breath. We recommend not doing any yoga exercises that require you to hold the breath if you are a beginning scuba diver, because you don't want to habituate to breath retention. We do, however, recommend practicing Victorious Breath *(Ujayi Pranayama)*—long steady inhales and exhales with a gentle emphasis at the back of the throat. Try exhaling with a 'ha' sound, and then try exhaling the same way with your mouth closed to produce a whispery sound, almost like a subtle snore. This breath can be used throughout the entire pose practice. As you practice this breath, allow your chest and belly to expand without force as you inhale, and feel your belly and chest contract as you exhale.

In addition to Victorious Breath, we recommend that divers practice something we call Regulator Breath, which is a modified tai chi style of breath. Place the tip of your tongue at the back of your teeth, then breathe through your mouth. As you exhale, let your cheeks puff out gently. This action mimics a controlled way you can breathe while on a scuba system. As you practice your poses try at least a few poses with Regulator Breath—especially when holding a difficult pose—so you learn how to keep the breath steady during physical exertion while breathing through your mouth.

Just like in scuba diving, breathing is the foundation of your yoga practice. Begin your home yoga session with a few minutes of deep breathing to help the mind transition from what you might be doing in the future to what you are doing in the present. Later in this book you will learn more breathing exercises that you can practice anytime you like.

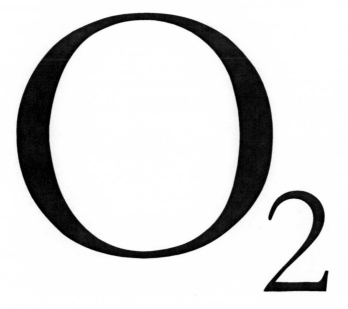

The chemical formula for molecular oxygen.

From birth, man carries the weight of gravity on his shoulders. He is bolted to earth. But man has only to sink beneath the surface and he is free.

—Jacques Yves Cousteau

Anatomy of a scuba diver

Overuse injuries can occur when people are not using the right muscles for the job or when they repeat movements beyond the point of muscle fatigue. Many people, for example, have weak gluteus muscles, so they rely on their knees for leg movements that ideally should originate with their hips, such as walking and finning. The hip joint is more powerful than the knee joint, but these people underutilize their hips and overuse their knees. If the motion of your legs while finning resembles riding a bicycle, you are not using the powerful muscles of the hip, which makes your strokes less efficient and causes more fatigue. However, you can strengthen the hips and other muscles, and retrain the body to move more efficiently, making diving more comfortable and enjoyable.

For diving, we focus on strengthening the following muscle groups:

- Gluteus muscles (the buttocks): There are three gluteus muscles which provide critical stability while moving around above water with your gear on, and when squatting to get your gear on and off. The largest and most superficial of the group—the gluteus maximus—is a prime mover for fin strokes.

- Quadriceps muscle group (front of the thigh): This four-muscle group works in concert with the gluteus muscles for helping you squat while weighted. The quadriceps group also keeps your knees straight when you fin which reduces drag through the water.

- Hamstring muscle group (back of the thigh): This three-muscle group helps you lower yourself down into a squat and stabilize you as you climb over large rocks and logs in full gear. They also assist finning by helping lift the leg from the downward stroke position.

- Hip flexor group (front of the hip and lower abdomen): This two-muscle group, called the iliopsoas, bends your hip. This group is also a prime mover for fin strokes, pressing the leg into the downward stroke position.

- Abdominal muscles (front of the torso): Several muscles in this group help stabilize the spine and are considered 'core' muscles. Without these muscles working properly, people will have problems staying prone under water and will often lilt to a side. Abdominal weakness also can lead to back pain. Muscles in this group include: the rectus abdominus, which are the long muscles through the center of the belly that define the classic 'six-pack' and bend your body forward; and the internal and external obliques, located on the sides of the abdomen, which enable you to twist and correct your stability when in a prone position under water.

- Back muscles (back of the torso): Several muscles in this group work with the abdominal muscles to stabilize the spine and are also considered 'core' muscles. Muscles in this group include: the erector spinae, which runs along your spine and helps you bend backwards; the rhomboids, which are in the upper back and help open the chest and maintain good posture; and the latissimus dorsi, which help pull the arm down and stabilize the back when carrying tanks. The smaller gluteus muscles in the hip and lower back area also work to support the spine. There are several other muscles that contribute to spinal stability, but these are the major ones for divers.

- Tibialis anterior (front of the shin): This muscle works to flex your foot. Because the design of fins causes you to point your toe the entire time you dive, the shin muscles can get overstretched and the calf muscles can get tight. By strengthening the shin muscles, you provide balance for the lower leg.

- Biceps (front of upper arm), triceps (back of upper arm) and anterior deltoid (front of shoulder): These muscles of the upper arm and shoulder enable you to carry heavy tanks on land. The biceps work with the anterior deltoid as you lift the tank from the ground and lower it without a crashing thud. The triceps muscles oppose the biceps and by strengthening both groups, you keep your elbow joint healthy.

Because of the nature of the activity, and the position in which divers hold their bodies for an extended period of time, divers are prone to tightness in several muscle groups. Holding muscles in one position for extended periods of time leads to cramps, and sometimes knotting in the muscles.

In addition to strengthening the previous muscle groups, divers should stretch these areas, especially after a day of diving:

- Pectoral muscles (chest), trapezius (upper back/shoulder/neck region), and levator scapluae (shoulder/neck): To counteract the load of the tank and dive weights, many divers hunch their shoulders forward and lift their shoulders up toward their ears. This hunching and rounding causes the chest muscles to tighten and the shoulder/neck area to stiffen. Your pectoral muscles work with the levator scapulae to draw your shoulders forward, and the upper portion of your trapezius works with the levator scapulae to shrug the shoulders upward. This area needs to be stretched after every dive.

- Hip flexors, quadriceps and gluteus muscles: If you are finning properly, you are using your hip flexors to bring your leg forward and your gluteus to bring it back; these muscles get used a lot in diving and need a good stretch afterward. Also, if you are finning with efficiency, you are holding your quadriceps firm to keep your knee relatively straight, which means the quadriceps are working constantly and need to release after a dive.

- Core muscles which stabilize the spine: After every dive you should move your spine in all directions, as it spent most of the dive in a limited range of motion—limited by an enormous tank of air strapped to it! The limited range of motion in your spine during diving can lead to muscle cramps. After every dive session, you should release your spine by moving it in the following directional planes: forward, backward, side-to-side, and rotation (a twist). We will cover the four directions in more detail as we go through the poses.

- Gastrocnemius and soleus muscles (in the calf): Fins are designed to work with a toe point, which means your calf muscles, and the Achilles tendon, are held in a contracted state the entire time you are diving. These definitely need to be stretched after a dive.

- Adductors (inner thigh) and hip abductors (outer thigh and hip): Your adductor muscles are found along the inner thigh. The abductor muscle group includes several muscles of the outer thigh and hip including the tensor fascia latae, gluteus medius and gluteus minimus. As you frog-style fin, you use your abductors to separate your knees and your adductors to draw your knees together. As you increase the range of motion of your hips, by stretching the inner and outer thighs, you can better perform a frog-style fin.

A good yoga pose practice incorporates both strengthening and stretching poses and a balance of work between front and back, left and right, and top and bottom of the body. When one muscle group is weak and the opposing muscle group dominates, this causes tremendous wear and tear on the joints. This makes it critical to both strengthen and stretch opposing muscle groups. For example, people who hunch their shoulders generally have weak, overstretched upper back muscles and tight chest muscles. By strengthening the upper back muscles and stretching the chest muscles, you can balance the two for better posture.

We have included a basic anatomy diagram to help you locate the various muscles we discuss for yourself. There are approximately 639 muscles in the human body; we obviously did not include all of them, just the ones we believe are key to diving.

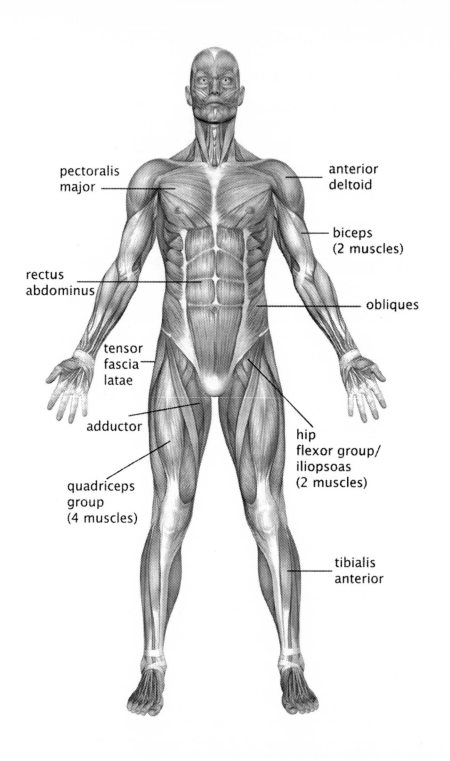

pectoralis major

anterior deltoid

biceps (2 muscles)

rectus abdominus

obliques

tensor fascia latae

adductor

hip flexor group/ iliopsoas (2 muscles)

quadriceps group (4 muscles)

tibialis anterior

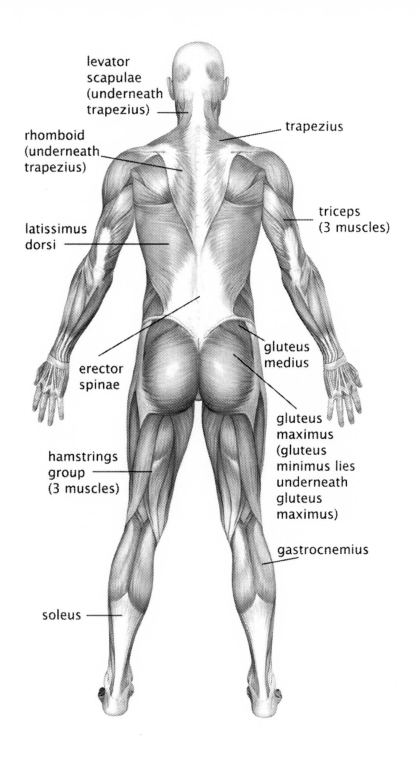

levator
scapulae
(underneath
trapezius)

rhomboid
(underneath
trapezius)

latissimus
dorsi

erector
spinae

hamstrings
group
(3 muscles)

soleus

trapezius

triceps
(3 muscles)

gluteus
medius

gluteus
maximus
(gluteus
minimus lies
underneath
gluteus
maximus)

gastrocnemius

Whatever you can do, or dream you can do, begin it. Boldness has genius, power and magic in it. Begin it now.

—Goethe

Preparing to practice

Despite some advertising to the contrary, you need only a very simple setup to practice yoga. You can practice yoga on your living room carpet, on the beach, in a park—wherever you can find a relatively flat, smooth surface with enough softness so you can tolerate kneeling, but not so much that it will bend your wrists. Some people purchase a sticky mat to help keep their hands and feet in place, but plenty of people practice without one. One thing we love about yoga is its portability—with a little creativity you can practice certain poses on a boat during surface intervals and on the beach before and after dives. There is no big financial investment to practice yoga beyond the cost of a book or some classes.

You can wear simple athletic clothing to practice yoga. In India, many people practice in their regular office clothing; however we advocate wearing something without belts, buckles or zippers because those can dig into the skin. Clothing need not be skin tight, but if it's too loose it can distract you. Traditionally you do the poses barefoot, so that you develop strength in your feet and ankles and you develop mechanical awareness in your stance. However, if you have foot problems and need to wear shoes, you can wear them for all of the standing poses. Most of the floor poses can be done in socks, but avoid wearing socks for the standing poses: it is too easy to slip in them.

Most recommendations call for practicing yoga an hour a day, but many people prefer to practice one hour a week. Others prefer to do twenty minutes a day. Consistency is more important than both intensity and duration, so evaluate your current schedule and carve out the time you can allot to your practice. This book is geared towards helping you create your own yoga practice, but we highly recommend joining a weekly yoga class so you get alignment help from an instructor.

Many traditional yogis say that 4:30 in the morning is the ideal time to practice yoga. That time may be ideal, but it's not very realistic for people with jobs, children, and other obligations. Morning is a great time to practice yoga because your mind is usually clear after a refreshing rest, but an evening yoga session can work wonders in transitioning from a busy workday to a time of rest. Some people split their practice into a short morning wake-up routine and an evening wind-down routine. Just make sure you wait at least an hour after a meal before doing a rigorous practice and drink a glass or two of water at least 90 minutes before your practice so your body is well hydrated.

Basic guidelines

Yoga practices strive towards balance, both on a philosophical plane and a physical plane. A balanced yoga pose practice works all sides of the body more or less equally. In structuring a yoga class, teachers focus on balancing the directional movement of the spine. If you can remember to do the following things, you have a well-balanced yoga pose practice:

- Bend forward
- Bend backward
- Twist side to side
- Bend side to side

For everything you do on the right side, you also do on the left. We demonstrate many single-sided poses in this book, so make sure you do both sides. You should do a relatively equal number of forward and backward bends and incorporate both strengthening and stretching poses for both the upper and lower body. In terms of sequencing, you want to warm up the spine gently at first, with something like Cat/Cow and warm up the large muscle groups of the arms and legs with poses such as Plank or Chair. You want to move from more subtle bends such as Downward Facing Dog to bigger bends such as Seated Forward Fold.

The time duration of each pose will vary, but we recommend holding the strength-building active poses for roughly four breaths and the more relaxing stretching poses for roughly eight breaths. However, you can flow between many poses, such as in the Sun Salutation sequence, which we will describe next. When you flow between poses you move with every inhale and exhale.

In yoga, we emphasize the effort, not the final result of the practice; if you can't touch your toes today, then maybe you will tomorrow, or the next day. The time you take to practice will benefit you, even if you never touch your toes. Our intention with the pose demonstrations is not to impress you with acrobatics, but rather to demonstrate poses that people with average strength and flexibility can do. Average does not mean everyone, so there will be some poses that come rather easily to you, and some poses that will confound you. Be patient with the process. Remember that you want to find your edge between work and pain in each pose; if you feel pain in a pose, modify it or skip it.

Physical fitness is not only one of the most important keys to a healthy body, it is the basis of dynamic and creative intellectual activity.

—John Fitzgerald Kennedy

Yoga poses for divers

This section discusses the various yoga poses that are beneficial to scuba divers. There are thousands of poses in yoga, but we've chosen the ones we think are most appropriate by analyzing the movements in scuba diving, along with our own physical experiences, to create this list. We have listed the Sanskrit names of the poses in parentheses, as you will hear these names used often in yoga classes and you will find these names used on many Web sites. After introducing each of the poses, we will provide you with recommendations for the application of the poses, such as pre-dive or post-dive.

For some of the poses, we have provided modifications and options. As you experiment with each pose, you should find the place where you feel work, but not pain. If a pose feels painful, particularly in the joints, you should either modify the pose or replace it with another pose that works the same area in a different way. Many people modify poses by using a chair or a wall for support. For example, they will place one hand the wall while practicing balance poses for additional support, or they will place their hands on the seat of the chair—instead of the floor—for many arm-strengthening poses to avoid pain in the wrists. You might also want to keep a necktie, small towel, or old sock handy to extend your arms in various stretching poses as well.

There is no shame in modifying poses; in fact, as both of us have dealt with various injuries over the years, we have had to modify our practice numerous times. Every body is different and the important thing is that you practice safely and stay in tune with what your body is doing throughout the practice.

Sun Salutation (*Surya Namaskara*)

Sun Salutations are sequences of yoga poses that flow together to provide you with a well-rounded routine. In this manual we will show a variation of a Sun Salutation that has been modified to avoid jumping into the poses. We will discuss the benefits of each pose after its description in the sequence. The overall benefit of a Sun Salutation is that it provides a balance of poses and is a good way to jump-start your day or warm up before beginning an activity such as scuba diving.

Classically, Sun Salutations are performed in the morning, as a greeting to the sun. They are invigorating for the body, which makes them great as a way to start your yoga practice. You can also use this sequence whenever you need a quick way to get your blood flowing and your energy level up.

One wonderful benefit to the Sun Salutation is that you follow each backward bend with a forward bend for balance, which takes the guesswork out of developing your own sequence. Even though these poses work well as a cohesive group, you can also practice any of the poses in the Sun Salutation sequence individually.

As you move through a Sun Salutation, you move into each pose on either an inhalation or an exhalation. We have marked each pose accordingly. As you extend the spine, or bend backwards, you inhale, and as you flex the spine, or bend forwards, you exhale. If a certain pose feels particularly beneficial to you as you move through this sequence, you can also stay in that pose for a few breath cycles before moving on.

Mountain *(Tadasana)*

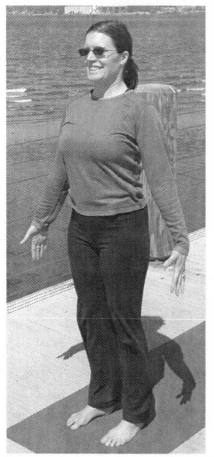

Begin the Sun Salutation in Mountain Pose, with the feet hip-width apart. Line up the heel of each foot behind its second toe, which means that most people will need to turn their heels outward slightly. Contract your quadriceps to straighten your knees without locking them. Pull your belly in to draw your hips slightly forward and lengthen your lower back—it will feel like you are pointing your tailbone towards the floor. Contract the muscles in the back of the hips for stability.

Lift your chest up away from the hips and draw your shoulders back without completely arching your upper back—if your ribs start to pop forward, you've drawn back too far. Drop your shoulders away from your ears; you will feel a contraction in the lower portion of the trapezius muscles along the middle of your back as you do this. Let your hands rest alongside your hips, with the palms facing either inward or forward.

Pose Benefits: Mountain Pose trains the body to stand correctly and keep the spine in neutral alignment. By focusing on head-to-toe alignment while standing in Mountain Pose, you can teach the body to keep the arches of the feet lifted while standing, and to engage the quadriceps to support your weight. By training the body to utilize your muscles to support your posture while standing, you better equip your back to handle the stress of supporting the additional burden of tanks and weight belts. This is a great pose to practice while standing around during a surface interval, or even while standing in line at the grocery store.

Upward Reach *(Hastasana)*

From Mountain Pose, inhale as you reach your arms overhead. You can have a slight arch to your upper back, making this a gentle back bend.

Use the same alignment for Upward Reach that you did in Mountain Pose. Line up the heel of each foot behind its second toe, which means that most people will need to turn their heels outward slightly. Contract your quadriceps to straighten your knees without locking them. Pull your belly in to draw your hips slightly forward and lengthen your lower back; it will feel like you are pointing your tailbone towards the floor. Contract the muscles in the back of the hips to help stabilize the pelvis. As you open the chest, avoid arching the lower back.

As your arms extend overhead, lift your chest up away from the hips and draw your shoulders back without completely arching your upper back—if your ribs start to pop forward, you've drawn back too far.

Pose Benefits: Upward Reach provides a gentle opening for the chest, which allows your lungs more space to expand as you inhale. Divers need to learn full complete breaths; by opening the chest like this you create more room for the lungs to expand to their natural fullness. This pose also has a good lengthening effect on the spine.

Forward Dive

From Upward Reach exhale as you bring your arms out to the side, and bend your knees as you dive your chest towards the floor, coming into Forward Fold. You may see people perform this with the arms extended overhead, but that puts more pressure on the lower back, which is why we advocate extending the arms to the side instead. By bending the knees a lot as you dive to the floor, you protect the lower back by allowing some slack in the hamstring muscles. The hamstrings connect from the lower back all the way down to the knee; unless you have excellent hamstring flexibility, keeping the knees straight means your hamstrings will tug on your lower back. You may see some people perform

this dive with straight legs, but we find bending the knees much safer for the lower back, and much stronger for the legs.

As you dive, keep the belly contracted and the spine long. The thigh muscles engage as you bend the knees. Feel your heels anchor into the floor and the arches of your feet lift. Your head is the last thing to descend.

Pose Benefits: Forward Dive is really a transition from standing to Forward Fold. However, by correctly engaging the abdominal muscles and the leg muscles as you fold, you can train the body to use these muscles and not rely just on the erector spinae to do all the work when bending over. As you gather your gear, you constantly stoop down; by practicing correct alignment in Forward Dive, you can learn to bend over to pick up your gear with stronger support for your back.

Forward Fold (*Uttanasana*)

Finish your exhale as you use Forward Dive to come in to Forward Fold. As you hold this pose, keep a gentle bend in the knees, and reach your belly towards your thighs. If you hold Forward Fold for several breaths, you can begin to straighten the knees gently. Keep an engagement in the lower belly, drawing it inward towards the spine to support the back. Point your tailbone towards the sky and keep the arches of the feet lifted.

Let your head completely hang and let your neck relax. Much tension accumulates in the neck throughout the day, and we can often see that tension still grip in this pose. Allow your head to hang like a useless dead weight, with the top of your head pointed downward.

If you hold this pose for several breaths, you can cross your arms and hold your opposite elbows. Another option, if in reach, is to clasp the back of your ankles and lightly pull your chest further down your legs.

Pose Benefits: Forward Fold lengthens the hamstrings along the back of the thighs while also stretching the lower back. Your hamstrings assist the gluteus maximus in lifting your leg up while finning. These muscles get tired and tight after a dive, which makes Forward Fold excellent for divers. This pose also provides some traction for the neck, helping to lengthen and release tight muscles of the neck.

Monkey *(Urdhva Mukha Uttasana)*

From Forward Fold, inhale as you come halfway up. Place your hands on your shins and extend your spine, coming into Monkey.

In Monkey, keep your spine long and straight, and have a slight bend to your knees. Maintain a subtle engagement of your lower abdominals and a slight squeeze of your shoulder blades to lengthen the spine. Your eyes should look several feet in front of you on the floor, keeping your head in line with your spine.

Pose Benefits: Monkey extends the spine and helps build excellent postural muscles by engaging the rhomboids of the upper back. Monkey builds muscles to sit up properly. It also provides some lengthening for the hamstrings in the back of the legs. Monkey teaches you to extend your spine, and the more you practice this pose the more your spine will automatically extend, even under water. This extension will help you feel more comfortable while diving.

Forward Fold again

After inhaling into Monkey, exhale back down into Forward Fold.

Lunge *(Anjaneyasana)*

From your second Forward Fold, inhale while stepping the left foot back into Lunge. Keep your right knee square over the right ankle; if the right knee reaches beyond your toes, hop back several inches until the right knee lines up over the ankle. This alignment is critical to avoid overstretching ligaments and tendons in the knee joint. If you maintain the arch in your right foot, it will help you better align your knee.

Keep the back knee straight and extend strongly through the back heel. Squeeze the back of the hips for stability. Try to balance without using your hands for support by hovering your fingertips just above the floor. Instead of flopping your upper body onto your thighs, feel the abdominal muscles engage to create a lift in the torso.

You can hold in Lunge for several breaths if you like. We have provided photos of several Lunge options. If you find balance difficult in Lunge, you can drop the back knee to the floor. If you want to challenge your balance more, you can sweep the arms overhead. Remember that if you lift your torso, keep the lower back long by engaging the abdominal muscles.

Pose Benefits: Lunge opens the hip flexor muscles in the front of the hip. These muscles are one of the primary movers in finning, so they contract a great deal during diving. Tightness in the hip flexors leads to an overarched lower back and often back pain. This makes Lunge a good post-dive stretch. Lunge also requires strong gluteus muscles, which are another primary mover in finning. Finally, Lunge also trains you to have good knee and ankle alignment, which helps to prevent injuries.

Lunge continued (pose options)

Downward Facing Dog *(Adho Mukha Svavasana)*

From Lunge, exhale as you place the hands on the floor, and step the front foot back next to the back foot to come into Downward Facing Dog. Place the hands shoulder-width apart, middle finger facing forward and fingers spread wide. Push forward into the fingertips to take the pressure off the wrist. Keep your arms straight and hang your head so your ears fall between your upper arms. Squeeze the lower trapezius (midway down your back) to pull your shoulders towards your hips. Broaden your shoulders away from the center of your spine.

As you maintain a gentle bend in the knees, reach your hips as high up and as far back as you can. You can bend your knees quite a bit to avoid rounding the spine. Your heels may or may not touch the floor, but continue to reach your heels towards the floor. Contract the front of your thighs to lengthen the back of the legs. Keep your belly pulling in gently. You can hold here for a while and alternate bending the right knee and pushing the left heel towards the floor, then switching sides, to stretch the calf muscles.

Downward Facing Dog continued

Bend your knees as much as you need to in Downward Facing Dog to keep your spine lengthened.

Pose Benefits: Downward Facing Dog is one of the most frequently performed poses in yoga because it works so many areas of the body. It provides traction for the entire spine, lengthening from head to tail. Many people consider this pose the best stretch for the back. The chest and shoulders open in Downward Facing Dog while the triceps of the upper arms and muscles surrounding the shoulder joint gain strength. This pose also provides a good opening for the hamstrings. For divers, the most important aspect of Downward Facing Dog is the excellent stretch this provides for the calf muscles, which stay in a contracted state the entire time you dive due to the design of fins.

Plank *(Dandasana)*

From Downward Facing Dog, inhale and shift your weight forward so your shoulders line up directly over your hands to come into Plank.

Keep your belly and your legs strong here so that the hips are slightly lower than your shoulders, as though your body were a stiff board propped against a wall. Draw your belly in and up, as if you were sucking your bellybutton into your spine. Push into each knuckle of your hands evenly. Your upper back should stay smooth and broad, without rounding the shoulders nor dipping the chest—to accomplish this, find a balance between the pectoral muscles in the chest and the rhomboids and latissimus dorsi in the back. Extend back through your heels to keep the focus of Plank as a lengthener from head to heel. Squeeze the gluteus maximus in the back of the hips strongly and engage the quadriceps so that the legs help support the body in Plank.

Plank continued

You can keep the integrity of the spine in Plank by dropping the knees to the floor, making it a Kneeling Plank. Note that Kneeling Plank is different from a classic "all-fours" position in that the shoulders line up over the hands, but the knees line up several inches behind the hips.

Pose Benefits: Plank is the ultimate core strengthener as it strengthens just about everything from shoulders to hips. This pose really teaches us how to engage our abdominals and hips for support. It also builds great strength in the chest and triceps. Plank serves as a good balance for divers because diving uses primarily the lower body, and this provides upper body strength. This pose also helps develop gluteus maximus muscles, which give divers their power while finning.

Hover *(Chatturanga Dandasana)*

From Plank, exhale as you shift even more forward so your shoulders are just beyond your fingertips. Bend the elbows straight back, and drop so you hover a few inches above the floor in Hover.

Squeeze the gluteus muscles tight and draw your belly in and up. This pose nearly mimics Plank, except that your torso is lower to the floor, your elbows are bent, and your hips are nearly level with your shoulders. Point the elbows straight back, so that your upper arms brush the ribs, which keeps the elbows in a natural alignment with the shoulders and wrists.

You can drop your knees to the floor to keep the integrity of the spine as you develop upper body strength.

Hover continued

Pose Benefits: Hover looks like a push-up starting position. It builds core strength, along with great strength in both the biceps and triceps as you lower into Hover and as you push out into the next pose in the sequence. This might seem odd at first, but divers do in fact need good biceps strength—anyone who has ever carried a scuba tank can attest to the need for strong bicep muscles. By moving slowly in and out of Hover, you use your muscles rather than rely on momentum to do the work.

Upward Facing Dog *(Urdva Mukha Svavasana)*

From Hover, inhale and turn the tops of your feet onto the floor, keep your knees up with your thighs off the floor, and press into your feet. Lift your chest and draw it forward between your arms to open for Upward Facing Dog. Only your hands and feet should be touching the floor. Use your quadriceps muscles to hold the thighs strong and press into the feet—this helps the lower back maintains its integrity. Your lower back will arch, but it should not feel like an extreme arch. Actively draw your shoulders down away from your ears; or, if it makes more sense this way, lift your head and neck up out of your shoulders like a turtle pulls its head from its shell.

Note that Upward Facing Dog can cause too much crunching in the lower back for some people. It can also strain the wrist joints. If this pose does not work for your body, move from Hover all the way down to the floor, and practice Cobra pose instead.

Pose Benefit: Upward Facing Dog is a back extension pose, which helps open the front of the body. It opens the hip flexors, which contract frequently during diving, and also opens the rectus abdominus (the central muscles of the stomach). Upward Facing Dog provides good balance and helps realign the spine, especially if you round your upper back frequently while wearing a BCD. This pose also strengthens not only your triceps in your upper arms but also your quadriceps in your legs when performed properly.

Cobra *(Bhujangasana)*

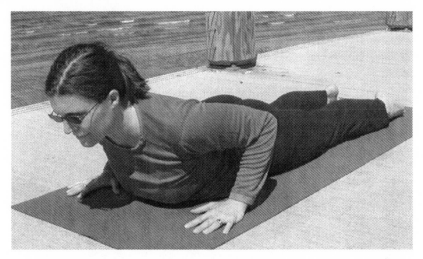

If Upward Facing Dog causes any lower back or wrist pain, then move through Hover to lower all the way to the floor on your exhale. On your inhale, keep the lower body on the floor, press very gently into the hands, with your elbows bent and pointing straight back, and lift the chest for Cobra.

While holding Cobra, keep your legs strong by activating the quadriceps muscles in the thighs and pressing your feet into the floor. Use a subtle abdominal contraction to ground your tailbone and keep the lower back long. Point your elbows straight back. Keep lifting the shoulders higher off the floor by using your upper back, not your hands. Try holding the pose for several breaths with your hands hovering just above the floor to make sure you are engaging your back.

Pose Benefits: Cobra pose strengthens the muscles of the upper back, such as the rhomboids, which helps you maintain good posture. Like Upward Facing Dog, this pose helps counteract the rounding of the shoulders many people do when they dive. This pose also engages the gluteus muscles in the hips as stabilizers for the pose. While this pose does not open the hip flexors like Upward Dog does, if you practice Cobra and Lunge in the same session, you can achieve the same type of opening for the front of the body.

Downward Facing Dog again

From either Upward Facing Dog or Cobra, push your tailbone up then flip your feet over so the balls of your feet press into the ground. Continue lifting your tailbone up and back to return to Downward Facing Dog during your exhale.

Three Legged Dog (*Eka Pada Adho Mukha Svanasana*)

From Downward Facing Dog, inhale as you lift the left foot high off the floor to come into Three Legged Dog. Hold the same alignment of the torso in Three Legged Dog as in Downward Facing Dog with the palms pressing evenly into the earth, the spine elongated, and the shoulders spreading outward. Keep both armpits facing the floor evenly. Extend strongly through the left leg and flex the foot by pushing through the heel to open the calf muscles.

Pose Benefits: Three Legged Dog is a preparatory pose to complete the Sun Salutation and bring you back into a Lunge. If you hold the pose for several breaths, it has the added benefit of making the upper body work a little harder, as you have one less limb to bear the weight in this pose. Three Legged Dog allows you to get a bit deeper into the calf stretch on the standing leg than you do while in Downward Facing Dog. In your beginner scuba classes, your instructor probably told you that divers most often cramp in their calf muscle, which makes this a creative recovery pose after diving.

Leg Swing

From Three Legged Dog, as you exhale, contract your stomach and round your back drawing your left knee forward. Swing the left foot all the way between your hands, moving through the Leg Swing to come into a Lunge with the left foot forward and the right leg back. This will take some practice. At first, you can use a lot of momentum by swinging quickly into Three Legged Dog and quickly out of it into the Lunge. After lots of practice, you eventually can perform this slowly; the more you engage the abdominals and round the back, the easier it is. To practice, you can try holding half way, lifting the knee high up towards the chest.

Pose Benefits: This Leg Swing, which is a transition pose to get from Three Legged Dog to a Lunge, builds great stomach strength. Strong abdominals created in this Leg Swing help support your back, especially when carrying a heavy weight belt. The more you engage the rectus abdominus and round the back, the more room you have to swing your leg through.

Lunge and Forward Fold again

Use the Leg Swing to swing your left foot forward into Lunge. Inhale and pause here in Lunge; you can sweep the arms overhead here as you inhale.

Exhale as you step your back foot next to your front foot coming back into Forward Fold.

Some people might find it easier to skip the second Lunge and just walk the feet forward from Downward Facing Dog back into Forward Fold. There's nothing wrong with using that transition to make your way out of the Sun Salutation.

Reverse Forward Dive to Upward Reach

From Forward Fold, inhale as you bring your arms out to the side, and bend your knees as you bring the body back to standing, coming into Upward Reach. This mimics the Forward Dive you used at the start of the Sun Salutation. As you come back up, really bend the knees and anchor the heels into the floor to feel the strength of your legs lifting the body and the strength of your gluteus maximus draw your torso upright. As in Forward Dive, keep the stomach strongly contracted.

Finish your inhale as you come into Upward Reach.

Chair *(Utkatasana)*

From Upward Reach, exhale as you bend at the hips and knees, pushing your hips way back to come into Chair pose. In Chair, feel your weight primarily in the heels of your feet; you can lift the toes to test their buoyancy. This pose mimics the act of sitting back into a chair. Keep your knees lining up with your second toe—often people will bulge their knees out in Chair; if that happens, squeeze the adductor muscles in the inner things to realign the knees. Maintaining arches in your feet will also help knee alignment.

To keep the lower back long and avoid crunching, suck your belly inwards and upwards with intensity and point your tailbone down towards the floor. You should definitely feel your abdominal muscles in Chair. Lift your chest up and draw your arms either straight out in front of you or overhead. Some people prefer to bend the elbows in Chair, or even rest the hands on the legs—find the hand position that works best for you. You can hold for a few breaths to build strength in the legs and hips.

Pose Benefits: Chair is also known as Intense Pose, and we concur. If you have difficulty climbing down to a shore dive site fully geared up, then this is the pose for you. Chair strengthens the quadriceps in the thighs, along with many hip stabilizer muscles, such as your adductors (outer thigh) and abductors (inner thigh). It also trains you to suck your stomach in strongly. You can tell the difference when you let your abdominal muscles go slack by placing a hand on your lower back—with slack abdominals you will feel an exaggerated arch in your lower back.

Chair continued (pose options)

Completing the Sun Salutation

From Chair, inhale as you come back into Upward Reach.

Exhale as you come back into Mountain Pose.

After doing one round of the Sun Salutation with the left leg stepping back first, repeat the entire sequence with the right leg stepping back first to ensure that you are even.

Note that as you go through the Sun Salutation, you can hold poses longer if you like; you can also add in more standing poses to create your own variation. Just remember to move with the breath and with control.

Sun Salutation benefits

By practicing the poses together in this sequence, you get a reasonably balanced practice. This sequence was developed so that each time you bend the spine forwards, you follow it with a backward bend for balance. To complete your practice, you would need to only add a side bend and a twist.

The Sun Salutation also lets you experience rhythmic breathing, as you move with the breath. At first, you may try to rush or lengthen the breath to match your movement, but over time you will learn to breathe naturally and move at the pace of your breath. This synchronization of breath and movement will help you tremendously when you dive. If you have ever taken a buoyancy training class, you know that you inhale to slightly ascend and exhale to descend. By practicing the Sun Salutations, you can develop that same breath control awareness that will help you tweak your buoyancy under water.

Other standing poses

In addition to the Sun Salutation poses, there are numerous standing poses that you can perform. Many of these standing poses develop strength, such as the Warrior poses, while other poses focus more on flexibility. When practicing the standing poses, try to hold each for roughly four complete breath cycles; some you will find easier to hold than others. Instead of only doing the poses that come easily, you should practice the ones you find more difficult, remembering the distinction between work and pain. When you find yourself struggling to breathe in a pose, back off from the pose a bit and try going to slightly less than your full range of motion in the pose.

We also chose to include several balance poses. At first you might wonder why we focus on land balance since divers perform their activities under water, where balance is not much of an issue. However balance is important for two reasons: 1) even though you dive under water, you spend quite a bit of time gearing up on land, stepping over other people's equipment on a boat dive or big rock formations on a shore dive—this requires tremendous balance; 2) mastering balance on land involves subtle engagement of core muscles and the ability to recruit the right muscle groups—the ability to control your buoyancy under water requires the same subtle engagement of core muscles and the ability to make small isometric contractions. The more you master these skills on land, the more muscle memory you will develop and the more automatic these subtle adjustments will become.

We advocate practicing a mix of standing poses and floor poses regularly. Practicing at least one balance pose every session will help you develop great muscle recruitment. As you practice the standing poses, feel free to practice near a wall or near a chair so that you can use some external support when you need it. Many people learn balance poses by practicing them at a wall for several sessions first.

Warrior 1 *(Virabhadrasana 1)*

Enter this pose from a Lunge and turn your back heel in approximately 30 degrees, placing your back foot flat on the floor. Keep the arches of both feet lifted. Your back toes should point at roughly one o'clock. Ideally, you should be able to draw a line from your front heel all the way through the arch of your back foot, but if that throws your balance off too much, you can stagger your feet a bit more. Keep the front knee bent and lift your torso up; you can support yourself by placing your hands on your thigh to come up. Contract your abdomen, particularly below the navel, so that your lower back does not over-arch. Engage the gluteus muscles strongly, particularly in your back leg. Unlike in other poses where you make it safer by bending the knees, the angle of the back leg in Warrior 1 makes it critical to keep the back knee straight without locking it.

Your can rest your hands on your hips, or bring them overhead, or even clasp your hands behind your back to open your chest. Maintain some space between your ears and your shoulders, but if you bring your arms overhead, let your shoulders rise slightly to accommodate their natural movement. In this pose, draw the elbows back and think about opening the armpits to create space in the chest.

Pose Benefits: Warrior 1 helps strengthen gluteus muscles in the back of the hip and opens up the hip flexors in the front of the hip. It's also a great opener for the pectoral muscles in the front of the chest. Warrior 1 helps divers counteract all the forward rounding that we tend to do while in our dive gear.

Warrior 1 continued (pose options)

Warrior 2 *(Virabhadrasana 2)*

Enter from Warrior 1. Your feet can stay in the same spot as in Warrior 1, but generally most people like to step their back foot about another six inches back. Rotate your torso and hips towards your back leg so that your shoulders and hips face the side. Keep your front knee bent up to 90 degrees, making sure the knee stays square over the ankle—if you look down, you should be able to see your big toe, but no other toes. Many people need to slide their knee more to the outside to find correct knee alignment.

Keep your hips lined up under your shoulders and the lower back in neutral alignment by drawing your abdominals inward. You should feel your hips pulling forward and slightly upward. Or, if this makes more sense: don't stick your butt out in this pose. Strongly stretch the arms straight out to the sides, engaging the triceps muscles and extending through the fingertips. Look just past your front fingertips with a focused gaze.

Warrior 2 continued

Pose Benefits: Warrior 2 is a great leg strengthener. It also opens the hips by stretching the adductor muscles (inner thighs); this stretch provides you with the flexibility you need for frog-style finning. It also stretches the bicep muscles in the arms as you extend strongly. Many of us keep our biceps in a contracted state when we dive by folding our arms, so this pose can help bring some extension back into the elbow joint. Warrior 2 can also help you maintain focus and intensity by practicing a focused gaze.

Extended Angle *(Utthita Parsvakonasana)*

Enter from Warrior 2. Your legs can stay in the exact same position. Drop your front arm onto your front thigh (the front leg is the leg with the bent knee). Rotate the top shoulder and top hip back, as if you are turning your heart and bellybutton to face the sky. Press strongly through the outside edge of the back foot and keep the front knee square over the ankle.

Your top arm can reach straight up, or you can bring it over the head with the palm facing down. You can also rest your top arm on your lower back. Keep some distance between your ear and your shoulder in the bottom arm. Your bottom arm can rest on the thigh, or you can lightly touch the fingertips to the floor if you can reach it without turning your chest downward. To make this Bound Extended Angle, you can wrap your top arm around your back and thread your bottom arm between the thighs to clasp your hands. Use a necktie or a long sock if your hands do not touch easily or if you have to turn the chest to touch hands. You can turn your head to look up, or just let the neck relax.

Pose Benefits: Extended Angle is the first side-bending pose that we have introduced. Bending the spine to the side is one of the four directions of spine movement that comprises a balanced practice. Extended Angle provides a great stretch through the waist and the latissimus dorsi muscles of the back. As in Warrior 2, Extended Angle enables hip opening, which is useful in frog style finning. If you make this a Bound Extended Angle pose, you help create greater mobility for the shoulders, which tend to stay fairly rigid while diving.

Extended Angle continued (pose options)

Triangle *(Trikonasana)*

Enter from Warrior 2. Keep the feet in the same position but straighten your front knee. Squeeze the quadriceps strong in both legs so the knees stay straight but without locking them. Your front heel should line up with the arch of your back foot, but you can stagger your feet slightly if balance becomes difficult.

Reach with your front hand as far forward as you can, stretching through the armpit, then bend to the side, bringing the forward hand to rest on your thigh, your shin, or the floor. The goal in Triangle is not to touch the floor, but rather to create length in the spine, so instead of thinking 'down', think 'out' as you reach.

Keep stretching through the waist on both sides and avoid rounding the bottom rib cage. Imagine pressing both shoulders and hips back against an imaginary wall—or try this pose against a real wall to maintain your alignment. Your top arm can reach straight up. You can turn your head to look up, or just let the neck relax. Often, we practice rotating the head in this pose to get movement back in the neck by inhaling to look up and exhaling to look down.

Triangle continued

If you find your shoulder cramping, you can rest your top arm on your lower back. If your neck begins to cramp in Triangle, you can turn your head to look down at the floor.

Pose Benefits: Like Extended Angle, Triangle is a side-bending pose that stretches the back laterally. We usually do not bend side to side while diving, and after a long day of diving Triangle helps reduce stiffness that can accumulate in our back. The difference between this pose and Extended Angle is that Triangle adds a stretch for the hamstring muscles in the back of the thighs, particularly on the front leg. Triangle also helps open the hips.

Standing Straddle *(Prasarita Padotttanasana)*

Enter from Triangle. Turn both feet so your entire body is facing the side. To measure the proper width of your legs, stretch your arms straight out to the side and your ankles should line up more or less under your wrists. Rotate your toes inward and heels outward—this is called pigeon-toed feet. Contract the front of the thighs to keep the knees straight. Whereas in many poses you can modify the pose by bending your knees, the angle of the knee in Standing Straddle requires you to keep the knees straight to protect them. You can modify this pose by taking your feet wider, or by facing a wall so you can touch your hands to the wall for support.

Cross your hands behind your back; if your hands do not reach, clasp a towel in your hands. As you exhale, bend from the hip—not the waist—keeping your back straight, as you lower your head towards the floor. Once you are down, you can release your arms, maybe touching the floor, or you can keep your hands clasped to open the shoulders. Some people prefer to keep their hands on their hips in Standing Straddle. If your head is nowhere near the floor, step your feet wider, but if your head rests easily on the floor, bring the feet closer together. Shift your weight forward so you feel heavier in the toes and lighter in the heels—this will keep your hips properly aligned with your ankles.

Pose Benefits: Standing Straddle stretches the hamstrings, calves and ankles. It also provides a gentle stretch to the erector spinae muscles in the lower back. If you keep your hands clasped, you open the pectoral muscles in the chest and the anterior deltoid in the front of the shoulder. While many standing poses build strength, Standing Straddle focuses more on the relaxing stretch aspect, which makes this pose wonderful for your post-dive recovery, especially if you had any challenging dives.

Standing Straddle continued (pose options)

Eagle *(Garudasana)*

Enter from Chair. Maintain the bend in your hips and knees and drop your hips as low as you can. Swing your left arm over your right arm, placing the left elbow on top of the right. Intertwine the arms, bringing either the back of the hands, or the palms, together; or just reach around and grab the shoulders. Draw the shoulders down away from the ears and extend the elbows up and away from the chest. Lift your left leg and cross it over the right leg. You can either wrap your left foot around your right calf or rest your left toes on the floor to the outside of the right foot.

Sit down as low as you can with your hips and bring your upper body back so the shoulders are directly over the hips. When you first get into this pose your chest will lean forward, but once you have your legs and arms squared away, slide your chest back so that your shoulders line up over your hips—this will help you balance better in the pose. Squeeze your elbows and knees together as you draw your abdominal muscles in.

Pose Benefits: Eagle adds great stability to your body's repertoire and challenges your body to balance on one leg, which is exactly what you do as you climb over rocks getting into the water. Eagle provides a great stretch for the upper back and shoulders. For the legs, Eagle stretches the muscles of the outer thigh and hip. It also releases the gluteus maximus muscles, which work hard while finning.

Eagle continued (pose options)

Tree *(Vrkasana)*

Enter from Mountain Pose. Stand firm on your left foot and come onto your right toes. Bend your right knee and open your knee out to the side, possibly out as far as a 90-degree angle. Keep your hips level. Slide your right foot up the inside of your left leg until your right heel pushes into the left leg either above or below the knee—avoid pressing your heel into your knee. Maintain a good arch in the feet and some dynamic tension between your right foot and your left leg.

Press your hands together in front of the heart, with the thumb at the sternum, or you can separate your hands and stretch them out overhead.

You can also do this pose by simply resting your right toes on the floor.

Tree continued

Pose Benefits: Tree increases your balance and stability. As you walk down to the beach carrying a huge tank on your back and step over a big rock, you are balancing on one leg. Tree also opens the front of the hip, creating the flexibility needed for frog-style finning. Out of all the balance poses, Tree has perhaps the most calming effect on the mind. If you have had trouble focusing recently, try holding Tree pose for a while to help clear your mind.

Dancer *(Natarajasana)*

Enter from Mountain Pose. Bring your right hand over head. Bend your left elbow and turn your left palm up, like a waiter carrying a serving tray. As you bend your left knee, keep your left palm facing up and pivot the left hand back to grab your left foot near the ankle. You should be grabbing the foot from the inside. If you cannot reach your foot, hold a necktie or small towel in your left hand and loop it around your left foot. Point your left knee straight to the ground and keep the left knee close to the body. Draw the left knee backwards and the left hip forwards to spread the stretch through the entire front of the thigh, rather than keep the stretch localized to the knee joint.

You can stand and balance here, and this is a great balance pose for you. If you feel stable, squeeze the back of your left hip and push your left foot into

your left hand, reaching the foot up and away from the body. Keep pushing the foot up and away to create space in the back of the left knee while still pointing the left kneecap towards the floor. For every inch that you raise the foot, drop your right arm and chest down in an equal amount. Dancer is perhaps the most difficult balance pose in this book; if you struggle with the balance, face a wall and place your right hand against the wall for extra stability. You can even practice on a boat by using the cabin walls for stability.

Dancer continued

Pose Benefits: Dancer strengthens the gluteus muscles in the back of the hip, while stretching the hip flexors and the quadriceps. The hip flexors and quadriceps get tight after a dive, which makes Dancer a great post-dive pose that opens up these muscles. Dancer also opens the pectoral muscles in the chest and the anterior deltoid in the front of the shoulder while providing a strong back bend for the spine. During a surface interval, you can practice Dancer for both the stretch of the muscles and the energy of the backbend.

Floor poses

In general, floor poses are done after the standing poses as you begin to cool the body. You can also use the more active of the floor poses, such as the Cat/Cow flow, as a warm up. Some of the floor poses are strengthening poses, while others are more stretching poses. You will find that when you bend forward, particularly in a supported stretching pose, such as Seated Forward Fold, you will find yourself relaxing. When you actively bend backwards, in a pose such as Camel, you will find yourself more energized. As you recall from our discussion of basic guidelines, a combination of forward bends, backward bends, side bends, and twists makes a complete practice.

We recommend combining a mix of standing poses with floor poses for balance. In general, you will hold a floor pose longer than a standing pose. We recommend holding a floor pose for roughly eight full breath cycles. Please note that some of the floor poses can put pressure on the kneecaps; placing a towel or a folded-up sticky mat underneath your knees can help relieve this pressure. Others feel pressure in the hips when lying face down; again some cushioning under the hips can provide relief. Remember that the poses originated with the term "comfortable seat," so even though you want to challenge the muscles, you should definitely make the bones and joints comfortable.

Cat/Cow (Bidalasana/Marjaryasana)

Enter from kneeling. Come onto hands and knees, with your knees directly under the hips and your hands directly under the shoulders. In general, people often spread themselves too wide in this pose, so it's often a good idea to have someone look at you from the side the first several times you practice to judge your alignment. Press firmly into the hands, keeping the triceps muscles of the upper arms strong. If this pose bothers your wrists, you can make fists with your hands and place your knuckles on the floor with the palms facing inward.

As you exhale, draw your bellybutton in and round your back, drawing your chin towards your chest—this is the Cat pose. As you inhale, arch your back, letting your belly drop towards the floor, squeeze the shoulder blades together and look up—this is the Cow pose. These poses are generally done together as a several-cycle flow to warm-up and balance the spine. You can add some articulation into this flow by moving from the tailbone first and allowing the movement to ripple up the spine; articulation does take some practice, but it helps you really slow down and move purposefully in this pose flow.

Cat/Cow continued

Pose Benefits: Cat/Cow is included in just about every physical therapist's prescription for back issues. This flow keeps the spine limber as you stretch it backward and forward in equal measures. If you do it slowly, you can get lots of flexibility in the spine and strength in the muscles that support it. This is a great pose to do after a day of diving to get movement back into the spine, which stays fairly rigid with an immobile tank strapped to it. Many people find Cat/Cow the best pose to do when they first wake up in the morning. Many yoga teachers use Cat/Cow to start their classes.

Spinal Balance

Enter from Cat/Cow. Draw your belly in and gently squeeze your shoulder blades so that your spine is neutral. Lift your right hand and reach your right arm straight out in front of you. Lift your left knee and push your left heel straight back. Flex your left foot by pointing your toes to the floor and extending through the heel. Your right hand should be no higher than your right shoulder and your left foot should be no higher than your left hip. Keep your hips level and your spine in a neutral alignment by drawing in the belly; you should feel like someone could rest a bowl of soup on your lower back without spilling it. After holding for several breaths, change sides and extend the left hand and right foot.

Pose Benefits: Like Cat/Cow, Spinal Balance is a pose that physical therapists often use for back strengthening. Spinal Balance requires you to coordinate core strength to help keep the spine neutral. The diagonal action of this pose has a lengthening effect on the muscles that support the spine. Massage therapists often look at diagonals when dealing with a patient—often if your right shoulder is tight, it will cause your left hip to be out of alignment. Spinal Balance helps correct these imbalances. Scuba divers need to develop strong coordinated core muscles because this coordination will keep your body neutral when diving. When you feel yourself tipping to one side while diving, you tap into these subtle core muscles to right yourself. The more you can develop the muscle awareness to hold yourself in a neutral balanced position, through poses like Spinal Balance, the less you will use your arms to maintain your position in diving and the more efficient you will become with buoyancy control and air consumption.

Boat (Navasana)

Enter from sitting. Draw your knees together and grab the backs of your thighs. Lift your chest and focus on lengthening the spine. Lift your feet an inch or two off the floor, keeping the knees bent at first. Begin to lift the feet and straighten the knees, as long as you can do so without rounding the back. Imagine your spine is like the mast of a sailboat; you want to keep it tall and

lifted. You can keep your hands on the floor, or grab the back of the calves, or reach your arms out to the side. Find the hand placement that allows you to hold the pose for several breaths without rounding the spine.

Note that your abdominal muscles may quiver in this pose because they are holding a strong isometric contraction while lengthening the muscle. Typically when you contract the rectus abdominus you shorten the muscle by rounding the spine, as in a stomach crunch. Boat pose asks it to maintain both length and strength simultaneously, which makes it challenging.

Boat continued

Pose Benefits: Boat is wonderful abdominal strengthener. It strengthens virtually all the muscles in the abdomen as well as lower back muscles. It also strengthens the hip flexors—the muscles used to draw your foot downward while finning. Strong abdominal muscles are essential to divers as they help the back carry a tank and extra weights. Strong abdominal muscles also help stabilize your spine so you avoid overarching your back while finning.

Camel *(Ustrasana)*

Enter from kneeling. You can place a folded up mat or a towel under your knees for extra cushion. Spread your knees hip-width apart, and align your feet directly behind your knees. Curl your toes so that the only part of your feet touching the floor is your toes. Make fists with your hands and place them on the very top of your hips. Press your hips forward, staying very strong in the front of the thighs and lift your chest up away from the hips, keeping length in the lower back. Squeeze your elbows towards one another to open the chest. Slide your jaw back first, then lift your forehead to look up at the sky and open the throat.

You can stay here with your Camel, or, if you can reach your heels without twisting, reach one hand at a time back and grab your heels. A good test to see if you are ready to reach back is to slide your right fingertips down the back of your right thigh and calf to reach your heels: if you can maintain contact with your leg without leaning back, then you are ready to grab your heels. You can also turn the tops of the feet flat on the floor while holding the heels to get deeper into the pose. Focus on the lifting and opening of the chest. Do not drop your head all the way back—always maintain some space between the back of your skull and the back of your neck to avoid crunching your cervical spine.

Note that this is a deep back bend, so come out of it very slowly and follow with a neutralizing pose, such as a Cat/Cow flow. You should only practice this pose once the muscles of your back have sufficiently warmed. A few flows in and out of Locust or the Cat/Cow flow can help prepare you for Camel.

Pose Benefits: Camel opens the hip flexors, which get used constantly while finning. It also opens the pectoral muscles in chest and shoulder muscles which get very contracted while carrying a tank. Camel provides a good lengthening for the abdominal muscles as well. This is a strong backbend, which makes it a great pose to do when you need some extra energy.

Camel continued

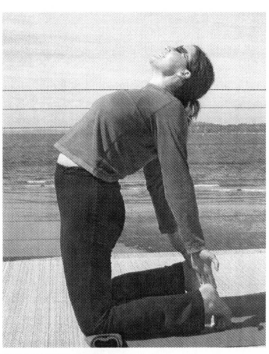

Child's Pose (Balasana)

Enter from Downward Facing Dog or kneeling. Come down onto hands and knees and spread your knees out a few inches; some people prefer the knees spread wide, while others prefer them closer—find the angle that makes your knees comfortable in this pose. Reach your hips back towards your heels and lower your chest towards the floor. Rest the hands back on the floor alongside the feet. Rest your forehead on the floor.

You can also stretch your arms forward with your hands on the floor for Extended Child's Pose. To make this pose more active, keep your elbows up; to make it more restful, let the elbows and forearms completely rest on the floor. If your head is nowhere near the floor, cross your arms and rest your head on your forearms. If you feel any discomfort in your knees, you can roll over onto your back and hug your knees into your chest instead.

Pose Benefits: Child's Pose is a wonderful stretch for the lower back, which takes a lot of abuse while carrying tanks on your back, sitting in airplane seats, and pretty much everything else we do. Child's Pose is also wonderfully calming for the mind, which makes it a great post-dive recovery pose, or even a pre-bedtime wind-down pose.

Child's Pose continued (pose option)

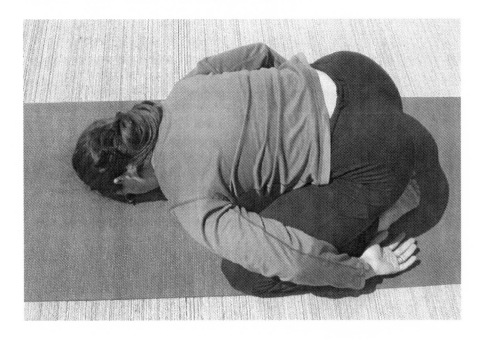

Seated Twist *(Bharadvajasana)*

Enter from sitting cross-legged. Sit very tall, feeling your spine elongate. Cross your arms and hold your elbows with the opposite hands. Exhale as you twist to the left using the strength of your oblique muscles in your abdomen. Inhale to come back to center. Exhale and twist to the other side. Repeat several times keeping your back very tall and your shoulders relaxed. Imagine your spine like a tall flagpole, and you are just rotating around that pole.

Once you have twisted side-to-side with your arms crossed several times, release your hands to the floor and hold the twist for eight breaths. As you hold the pose, try to keep both hips on the ground, the shoulders relaxed and the spine tall.

The chest should stay broad in this pose; feel yourself broadening your shoulders as you twist. When you hold on the other side, change the cross of your legs so that the opposite leg is in front for balance. Note that by habit, when you first sit down you will often cross your legs only one way, but it's a good idea to cross both ways so you create balance between your left and right hips and knees.

Seated Twist continued

Pose Benefits: Seated Twist is a spinal rotation pose. We have modified this twist slightly to make it easier on the knees, while still getting the benefits of rotating the spine. By adding this pose into your practice, along with forward bends, backward bends and side bends, you have a complete practice for the spine. Spinal rotation is critical after a long day of diving because it helps bring mobility back into a spine that has been immobilized by a tank for hours. This pose strengthens your internal and external oblique muscles—you use these muscles when you twist to look at something and, perhaps more importantly, you contract these muscles isometrically the entire time while diving to help stabilize you and keep you from tipping sideways. Developing these muscles will help you correct yourself instantly when you feel your body lilting to one side.

Locust *(Salabasana)*

Enter from lying face down. Stretch your fingers back towards your toes. Inhale as you lift your chest and feet as high as you can. Squeeze your feet towards one another as your point your toes and fingers back strongly. Feel your body extend from the crown of your head to the tips of your toes. Look straight ahead with your eyes. Instead of cranking the head to look up, lift the back of the skull so that the neck stays in line with the rest of the spine. You can either hold for several breaths or practice a flow by lifting as you inhale and descending as you exhale.

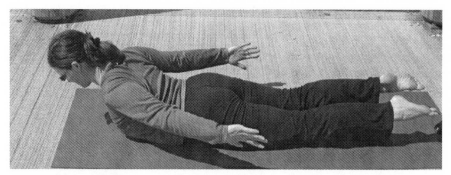

Pose Benefits: Locust strengthens almost all the muscles along the back of the body, making this an excellent pose to support a strong posture. It strengthens the hamstrings in the back of the legs and the rhomboids in the upper back. This backwards bend will help you maintain good posture, even with the weight of a tank distorting your normal center of gravity. As you practice this pose, you can imagine yourself hovering over a reef.

Pigeon *(Eka Pada Rajakapotasana)*

Enter from Three Legged Dog with your left leg lifted. Bend your left knee, drawing the knee close up to the chest using abdominal strength. This action is similar to the Leg Swing except instead of placing the left foot between the hands you will draw the left knee towards your left hand and bring the left foot towards your right hand. Once you get your left knee angled out to the side, rest the left shin on the floor and let the hips sink to the ground.

Some people like the knee closer in to the centerline of the body, some people like it more out to the side—adjust your foot and knee so that you have no knee pain. Wiggle your right foot back a few inches as you slide your hips backwards. The hips should more or less square to the ground. If they do not, place a towel or a pillow underneath the hip that is popping up so you can relax in this pose.

There are numerous variations of Pigeon you can do from here. If you want to stretch the hip flexors in the right hip, push your fingers into the floor and lift the chest.

Pigeon continued

If you feel stable in this position and want to add a quadriceps stretch, bend your right knee, drawing your right toes in towards your head as you grab your right foot with your right hand. Eventually, you may even be able to clasp both hands around the foot for what many people call Screaming Pigeon.

Many people enjoy relaxing in Pigeon to release the lower back and hips. To do so, come onto your forearms and let your head relax, resting your head either on your forearms or directly on the floor. If you do add the quadriceps stretch variation of Pigeon, follow it with this relaxing variation for a few breaths.

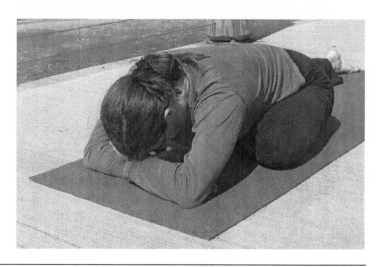

Pigeon continued

If this pose causes you knee pain try an Upright Pigeon instead. Sit up, rest your hands next to your hips, then bend your right knee and place your right foot on the floor, a few inches away from your hips. Cross your left foot over your right thigh, keeping the left foot flexed to protect the ankle.

Or, if you feel like resting more, you can take an Upside Down Pigeon. From Upright Pigeon, just roll onto your back while tucking your chin. Wrap your right arm around your right thigh and thread your left arm through the space between your legs. Gently pull the right thigh closer to your chest and move the left knee away from the chest. Keep the tailbone on the floor as much as possible. The right foot can circle in the air to stretch your ankle and foot.

Pigeon continued

    Pose Benefits: If we kept a list of most-requested poses, Pigeon would certainly make the top 10. Pigeon stretches the gluteus muscles in the back of the hip and lower back, and gets into some deep lower back and hip muscles that are hard to stretch, such as piriformis. These muscles of the back and hip may be deep, but are often a source of tremendous pain. People with sciatic nerve conditions often find this pose gives them relief. Divers constantly use their lower backs and gluteus while diving, so Pigeon is a great post-dive stretch. If you add the quadriceps stretch variation, you are getting a big back bend and a big stretch for the front of the thigh. Or, if you just focus on keeping your chest lifted, Pigeon is very effective for stretching the hip flexors. Pigeon is versatile, with many variations; it can be an energizing pose if you focus on the back bend, or a relaxing pose if you fold forward.

Cobbler's Pose *(Baddha Konasana)*

Enter from sitting. Bring the soles of your feet together several inches away from your groin, pressing the heels and the balls of the feet firmly together. Gently hold your feet or your shins. Keeping your spine straight, reach the chest forward, stretching out of the hips. Let your knees open towards the floor; you can put pillows under your knees to help the body relax further into the pose. Once you have reached as far forward as you can with a straight spine, you can allow the back to round forward. As you hold this pose, you can even give yourself a foot massage. This pose, technically called Bound Angle, is most often referred to as Cobbler's Pose because cobblers would sit like this with shoes wedged between their feet as they worked.

Pose Benefits: Cobbler's Pose stretches the inside of the hips and the inner thighs. When you do a frog-style fin, often used in wreck diving to avoid kicking up silt, you are constantly opening and closing the thighs with bent knees. You need hip flexibility to fin frog-style, and Cobbler's Pose helps you develop that. Also, this pose creates length in the spine and allows the back to relax. This is a relaxing forward bending pose, which can help you wind down at the end of the day.

Staff (Dandasana)

Enter from sitting. Stretch your legs straight out in front of you, pressing through the heels and pointing the toes straight up. You can have a slight bend in your knee. The goal in this pose is to sit up straight. If tightness in the hamstrings or your lower back prevents you from sitting up straight, sit on a folded mat or towel to elevate your hips. By elevating your hips, but not the rest of the leg, you can tip the pelvis forward enough to sit up straight. You can also try this pose sitting with your back against the wall to start and gradually develop the strength to hold this pose without using the wall.

Place your hands next to your hips and maintain some tension in your triceps muscles. If the length of your arms makes you hike your shoulders up towards your ears, bend your elbows slightly to keep your shoulders away from the ears. Lift the chest slightly and engage the abdominal muscles to maintain support. Slide your jaw back so your head is in line with the spine. Contract the quadriceps strongly.

Pose Benefits: In teaching, we often rename Staff as "Proud Sit" because it trains you to sit up tall and regally. Staff builds postural muscles so you can support the weight of tanks without strain. In this pose, you can definitely feel how the quadriceps help support good posture. Staff also strengthens the abdominal muscles. Staff and Plank share the same Sanskrit name because yoga was an oral tradition for centuries, which makes translations into English tricky.

Seated Forward Fold *(Pashimottanasana)*

Enter from Staff. Stretch your legs straight you in front of you, reaching through the heels and extending the toes to the sky. The knees can have a soft bend. Feel your pelvis slightly tip forward; if you cannot feel this action, then definitely elevate your hips so that you can originate this fold from your hips, not from your waist. You can place a folded mat or towel under your hips to help elevate them. Reach as far forward as you can while keeping your back straight. You can loop a small towel or necktie around the balls of your feet and while holding the towel in your hands, draw your elbows back and pull the chest forward—this technique helps maintain a long spine. Hold your extended spine for several breaths, and when you have gone as far as you can, you can begin to round the back and relax into the fold.

Seated Forward Fold continued

Because divers often get very tight calves while diving, we like to add a variation on this pose to emphasize the calf stretching aspect of it. Bend your knees a lot and grab the balls of the feet with your hands. Keep your heels on the floor and pull the balls of the feet towards your face. After several breaths, begin to straighten your knees while holding the grip. If you have difficulty holding your feet while straightening your knees, loop a necktie around the balls of your feet and use it for leverage.

Pose Benefits: Seated Forward Fold provides an excellent stretch for the hamstrings along the back of the thigh. It also helps lengthen the erector spinae in the lower back. Because divers point their toes the entire time they are finning, their calves get shortened, and the muscles of the shin can overstretch. By using the pose variation, you strengthen the tibialis anterior and stretch the calf muscles, bringing balance into your lower leg. The relaxing nature of this Seated Forward Fold also makes it a great post-dive pose.

Neck Stretch

You can do this pose either sitting or standing. This is not a yoga pose per se, but it's a wonderful thing to do. Grab your right wrist with your left hand and pull your right hand down towards the outside or your left thigh. Drop your left ear towards your left shoulder. You can rotate the head a bit until you feel a strong stretch.

Some people prefer to do the same stretch, only pulling the hand across the back of the body, which will better stretch the levator scapulae.

If you feel much tighter on one side of your neck, do that side first, then do the other side, then repeat the first side so you get to it at least twice.

Pose Benefits: Our necks take so much abuse in our daily lives. The upper trapezius muscles in the tops of the shoulders and the levator scapulae in the neck often overwork while diving because they have the weight of a BC and tank bearing down on them during the dive entries and exits. When trying to keep an ill-fitting rental BC on their body, or when they get cold, many divers shrug their shoulders up. The muscles of the upper trapezius and levator scapulae are responsible for elevating the shoulder blade. The upper trapezius muscles are notoriously tight and knotted up on many people, so this stretch should always be done after a long day of diving. This pose also helps relieve neck tension after a long uncomfortable flight to your dive vacation destination. In fact, you can do this simple pose on the airplane, even while crammed in the middle seat.

Lying Spinal Twist (*Jathara Parivartanasana*)

Enter from lying on your back. Bend your knees and place your feet flat on the floor. Square yourself so your shoulders and hips line up. Extend the left leg straight out along the floor, pointing the toes straight up in the air. Push your right foot into the floor enough to lift your hips and swing them two inches to the right, then place your right foot on top of your left thigh, just above the knee. Roll all the way over onto your left hip, letting the right knee descend towards the floor. While anchoring both shoulders down on the floor, stretch your arms straight out to the side. You can use your left hand to gently press the right knee closer to the floor. Placing a pillow underneath your right knee for support will help you release further into this pose.

Classically you would turn your head left in this pose, turning your head in the opposite direction of your knee, but you can also turn your head in the same direction—see how your neck feels that day and what feels best for you. Just make sure that when you change sides your head goes the other way so both sides of the neck get a stretch. Many people like to practice Lying Spinal Twist right before they end their practice with Corpse pose because it helps the back relax after all the hard work.

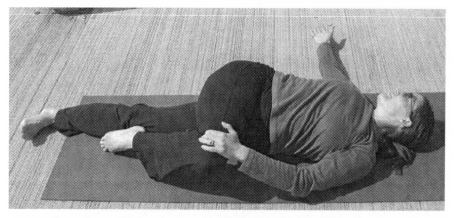

Pose Benefits: Lying Spinal Twist is another pose that rotates or twists the spine. Twists are thought to be cleansing poses by stimulating internal organs such as the liver and intestines in the same way that a massage stimulates muscle tissue. Lying Spinal Twist provides a passive opener for the pectoral muscles in the chest along with the gluteus muscles in the hips. This twist also provides a great release for the back. If we had to advocate one pose that divers should do after a long day of diving as a recovery pose, Lying Spinal Twist would probably be the one.

Corpse (*Savasana*)

Enter from Lying Spinal Twist. Bend your knees and bring your feet flat on the floor. Wiggle around a few times until you straighten out your spine. Stretch the legs out one at a time along the floor, then separate your feet several inches apart letting your feet flop out to the sides. Bring your hands on the floor, several inches away from the thighs away with the palms up. Allow your shoulder blades to rest flat on the floor. Take up as much space as you need to feel comfortable.

If you feel any twinges in your lower back, place some pillows under your knees to keep the knees bent and prevent tight hamstrings from yanking on your lower back. If you feel any neck tension, you can roll up a small towel underneath your neck, or even place your head on a pillow. Close your eyes and allow your entire body to sink into the floor. Notice your breathing become effortless. Let your mind slow down and permit thoughts to drift in and out of your mind like a half-knot current, without getting sucked into analysis. Try not to fall asleep in Corpse—you want to stay awake, yet peaceful and rested.

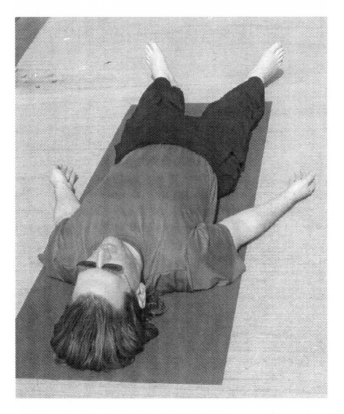

Corpse continued

Pose Benefits: Corpse is the most important pose in yoga because it enables your body to incorporate all the bending, twisting, stretching, and contracting that you have just done. You should spend 10 percent of your total practice in Corpse; so if you practice for 30 minutes, try to spend at least three of those minutes in Corpse. However, if you are just practicing a quick morning wake-up routine, you may want to substitute Mountain Pose for Corpse. When practicing the poses, it's important to end with a few moments of stillness: it gives your body the chance to record the muscle memory you just developed and, if nothing else, it gives your mind some well-earned downtime. Corpse is a useful pose to practice the visualizations that we describe later in this book.

Time and place for poses

We have listed numerous poses in this book that will get you started. As you take classes, rent DVDs, and read other books on yoga you will learn even more poses. The following is our recommendations for when to do the various poses; however, there is no right or wrong time for doing them. If after a dive you feel like doing a certain pose, then do it. The more you practice yoga the more you will intuitively know which poses your body needs at any given time.

Poses to do on a regular basis as regular conditioning

- Sun Salutations (and all the poses therein)
- Cat/Cow
- Warrior 1
- Warrior 2
- Triangle
- Extended Angle
- Tree
- Eagle
- Dancer
- Locust
- Boat
- Spinal Balance
- Seated Twist
- Staff
- Lying Spinal Twist
- Corpse

Good pre-dive warm up poses

- Sun Salutations (and all the poses therein)
- Dancer
- Triangle
- Cat/Cow
- Camel
- Seated Twist

Good post-dive recovery poses

- Extended Angle
- Standing Straddle
- Tree
- Eagle
- Pigeon
- Cobbler's Pose
- Child's Pose
- Seated Forward Fold
- Neck Stretch
- Lying Spinal Twist
- Corpse

Fin technique exercise

For some people, especially those who spent their childhood swimming, good fin technique comes naturally. But for many people, it requires developing a new motor skill. You can try this exercise at home to build up the muscle memory in your hips to fin properly. Physical therapists often use this exercise for people with knee problems to help strengthen the hips so that the knees don't bear the bulk of the work.

Stand sideways on a staircase, so that your feet are parallel with the steps and your right foot is on the outside of the step. Steady yourself by placing your left hand either on the wall in front of you or on the railing. Allow your right foot to hang over the edge of the step. Bring your left foot firmly near the edge of the step, practicing good form with your heel lined up behind your second toe. Bend your left knee slightly.

Keep your right knee straight and point your right toes, as if you were wearing fins. Contract your abdominals to lengthen the lower back. Using your hip flexor muscles, draw your right foot forward roughly two inches, then return the foot through center and draw it back two inches using your gluteus muscles. Keep the movement very small to begin as you move back and forth. Maintain a straight knee. Move slowly to avoid using momentum.

Take your right hand onto your lower back to test your curvature: as you draw the right foot back, your lower back may arch slightly, but you should not feel your lower back curling excessively as you move. If you find your lower back moving, make your leg swings smaller, engage your abdominals more, and try to focus on squeezing the back of the hip.

After you have done maybe 20 swings on the right leg, switch sides. Repeat this activity every day for a few weeks so your muscles can learn proper mechanics. Once you feel confident in this move, you can try it without bracing your arm on a wall or railing for support.

The highest form of maturity is self inquiry.

—The Reverend Dr. Martin Luther King, Jr.

Visualizations, meditation, and deep rhythmic breathing

Some consider meditation and visualization to be two separate things; we find them subtly distinct yet closely related. In the yogic tradition, visualization is akin to concentration *(dharana)*, and meditation *(dhyana)* is another limb. They both are similar in that they require several minutes of sitting still, plus slow, deep, rhythmic breathing. We believe visualization and meditation techniques are a wonderful benefit to a scuba diver's yoga practice. Visualization techniques, used by athletes for years, help you prepare for the dive itself, while meditation techniques help you maintain a sense of overall calm. Since most dive accidents can be traced to panic and poor judgment, the ability to relax under water is essential to divers. Deep rhythmic breathing is essential to meditation and visualization practices, so we have included breathing exercises in this chapter.

Note that meditative practices can sometimes cause you to face past issues, so it's possible that meditation can evoke strange emotional responses, dreams, and moods. Meditation holds a mirror up of your inner self and sometimes we see things we've tried very hard to ignore. Since modern society has so many distractions, we can spend days on end without any self-reflection, which makes a meditation practice so powerful. If you find yourself overwhelmed, seek counseling from either a professional or some trusted friends. Trust that you are not doing anything 'wrong' if you have some mixed feelings after a meditation practice.

Deep rhythmic breathing

Steady rhythmic breathing is the key to a good meditation practice. Before beginning your visualization or meditation practice, spend at least two minutes counting your breath without forcing it. As you move through a visualization or meditation practice, keep coming back to counting your breath as a way to center yourself. We recommend doing a count of "inhale 1-2-3-4, exhale 4-3-2-1." The important thing is consistency of the tempo and the ease of the breath—it should never feel strained or rushed.

Often people take shallow, barely noticeable breaths. But with deep breathing the entire torso should expand. The front, sides, and back of the chest should expand along with the belly as you inhale, and should passively contract as you exhale. Try imagining a balloon inside the torso expanding in three dimensions as you inhale, then deflating evenly towards the center as you exhale. However, deep breathing should feel effortless, not strained.

Deep rhythmic breathing is a great technique for dealing with stress under water—stop what you are doing and count your breath for a few cycles: "inhale 1-2-3-4, exhale 4-3-2-1". This will help you relax and will ensure that you are getting enough oxygen to your brain so that you can think clearly. Rhythmic breathing is a simple and powerful tool you can use to reduce anxiety, and by practicing frequently on land you will have this tool more readily available for when you need it under water.

You can practice deep rhythmic breathing anywhere—on an airplane, in traffic, just before bedtime, wherever. We do recommend that you maintain deep rhythmic breathing during your visualization practice.

Buddy breathing exercise

Some dive instructors teach buddy breathing to beginning students, while others only teach it to people in the divemaster training classes. You would use buddy breathing when you run out of air and your buddy does not have an alternate air source, requiring the two of you to share your buddy's one primary regulator. Buddy breathing requires not only excellent breath control, but also the ability to stay calm under pressure while coordinating a difficult task. We hope that all of your buddies dive with an octopus and that you never have to use this skill, but it's critical to be prepared because gear can fail. If you are interested in learning how to buddy breathe under water, we advise you to seek a certified dive instructor who can teach you the proper technique.

We have developed a simple breathing exercise you can use to practice the breathing rhythm at home. Relaxed buddy breathing works like this:

1. With the regulator, you inhale for four counts.

2. You exhale for four counts.

3. You inhale for four counts.

4. You pass the regulator to your buddy, continuing to exhale slowly, blowing tiny bubbles.

5. Your buddy inhales for four counts.

6. Your buddy exhales for four counts.

7. Your buddy inhales for four counts.

8. Your buddy returns the regulator to you.

Your buddy's breathing sequence while he has the regulator will be 12 counts; however, we recognize that it will take two counts for you to pass the regulator to your buddy and another two counts for your buddy to return it. This means you need to exhale continually for a full 16 counts. If you breathe slowly and calmly, you can relax your body and perform the skill with ease. But many people rush the breathing, which creates a vicious cycle of tension: the faster you breathe the more tense you become, the more tense you become the faster you breathe.

Practice this skill at home. We recommend using our Regulator Breath by placing the tip of your tongue at the back of your upper front teeth and allowing your cheeks to billow out as you exhale.

1. Inhale "1-2-3-4"

2. Exhale "4-3-2-1"

3. Inhale "1-2-3-4"

4. Slowly exhale "1-2-3-4-5-6-7-8-9-10-11-12-13-14-15-16"

5. Repeat the pattern for several cycles.

As you exhale for your 16-count, you can bring your lips closer together and just let the air seep out from the small gap between your lips, just as if you were blowing bubbles. This will help you extend your exhale to a count of 16. Keep your inhalations full, smooth and steady and avoid rushing them. Be patient with this breathing exercise, as this may take some time to develop. This exercise is a great buddy exercise as well: you can simulate on land by passing a regulator back and forth and pretending to breathe from the regulator.

The more you practice this exercise, the greater your maximum oxygen uptake (VO_2 max) becomes. Your VO_2 max is the maximum amount of oxygen your body can transport and consume, and is one sign of cardiovascular fitness. According to the Divers Alert Network (DAN), up to 30 percent of all diving fatalities each year are due to cardiovascular problems. Even if you never buddy breathe under water, practicing breathing exercises like this and engaging in aerobic exercise helps keep your cardiovascular system healthy so you can dive more safely.

If you had to do this skill in a real out-of-air emergency, it's likely that your buddy would not have the endurance to keep exhaling for the full 16 count, especially if he's the one who ran out of air. Recognize this, and build up to the longer breath counts by starting with just a 2-count inhale/exhale cycle; this would require only a 10-count exhale while the regulator is with your buddy. Encourage your buddy to relax, and slowly work your way up to longer breath counts. Once the two of you fully relax into the 4-count cycle, you'll be amazed at how calmly you can work yourself out of whatever problem you need to deal with before ascending together.

Visualization practice

In visualization, you use the technique athletes have used for decades. Visualizations let you see yourself succeeding, and many consider it a great training technique. Visualizations help you prepare yourself psychologically for a dive, and can be particularly useful if you are trying something challenging for the first time, such as wreck dive.

Before you begin, make sure you have at least 20 minutes blocked off in your day planner so you will not feel rushed. Visualization exercises also work very well after practicing the poses. Arrange a comfortable seated position that enables you to maintain a long spine, such as sitting on a pillow with your back against the wall. You can also practice in Corpse pose if you can do so without falling asleep.

Begin with your eyes closed, and count your breath, "inhale 1-2-3-4, exhale 4-3-2-1," keeping an even steady rhythm. We recommend using Regulator Breath as much as you can during your visualization session: place the tip of your tongue against the back of your teeth, as you would when cautiously inhaling with a regulator, and let your cheeks gently puff with each exhale through the mouth. When you feel your heart rate slow down, shift your concentration away from the breath and begin to work through the visualization. We have two suggested visualizations here to get you started; you may want to ask a friend to read these to you the first time you practice. These visualizations are suggestions to give you ideas for creating your own.

Visualization 1: Enjoying a smooth dive

This visualization serves as a great general dive preparation. We will describe this as a shore dive, but if you find yourself diving from a boat more often, then substitute the details of a boat dive for a shore dive. Also, we will describe some life found in the Caribbean, but you can substitute the aquatic life from either the region you most often dive, or the region you are traveling to on your next dive vacation.

Begin by imagining yourself standing on the shore with your wet suit on, but not quite zipped. As you calmly gather your gear together, express your excitement to your buddy about what you are about to see. See yourself zipping your wet suit and assembling your gear. As you and your buddy go through your pre-dive safety check, notice that everything is in order. As you walk from the bluff of the beach to the rocky entrance, feel your balance and your strength, and thank yourself for all that hard work in your yoga poses. As you and your buddy walk knee-deep into the water, feel the coolness of the water soothe your skin. Keep your breath flowing: "inhale 1-2-3-4, exhale 4-3-2-1."

You and your buddy calmly snorkel out to the dive site marked by a buoy. You encounter mild resistance, finning against the incoming tide, but with only a six-inch tidal exchange, you find it a simple task. As you and your buddy reach the buoy you look down to see the bottom visible through the clear turquoise water. Notice the waving palm tree branches and pink cottages of your resort as you take your land bearings. Smell the salt of the sea surrounding you. Keep your breath flowing: "inhale 1-2-3-4, exhale 4-3-2-1."

After making your checks and noting the time, begin your descent. Visualize the color changes and feel the temperature changes as you break through the first few feet. Feel your ears release as you equalize and slowly make your way down the line. You can even physically smile as you face your buddy. Keep your breath flowing: "inhale 1-2-3-4, exhale 4-3-2-1."

Find yourself coming to the reef and begin to observe the vast array of blues, purples, and other colors. Follow with your eyes tiny fish nibbling at the reef. Feel your hands clasp together; you don't need them to steady yourself because you're using your core muscles for that. Watch yourself begin to fin along the reef using long smooth, steady strokes, originating each stroke from your hip and maintaining a long torso. Keep your breath flowing: "inhale 1-2-3-4, exhale 4-3-2-1."

As you watch yourself and your buddy gliding over the reef, moving away from shore, feel your mind and body at ease as you gradually descend with the reef. Witness the various shapes, sizes, and colors of the fish. Watch the multi-colored and multi-striped fish move around you with both casual observance and guarded optimism. Notice the brilliant color of a blue tang, or the humorous stripes of a sergeant major. See yourself float above giant brain coral, using your breath to fine-tune your buoyancy; watch the fan coral dance with the gentle currents. Keep your breath flowing: "inhale 1-2-3-4, exhale 4-3-2-1."

Look with your mind at your depth and time and realize that you have reached the end of the dive. Since this is your first dive of the trip, and you wanted something uncomplicated, see yourself signaling to your buddy that it's time to turn around. Feel yourself maneuvering effortlessly under water and follow the contour of the reef back up to where you first descended. Stay calm and at ease, knowing you have plenty of air left because you kept the breath steady and calm. Keep your breath flowing: "inhale 1-2-3-4, exhale 4-3-2-1."

View the line now coming in to focus. Feel the roughness of the rope against your palm as you grip the line to steady yourself. Visualize you and your buddy ascending as calmly as you descended. See you and your buddy making a safety stop for a few minutes at 15 feet, bobbing gently in the water, watching the fish below. Finally, feel yourself slowly ascending and breaking through the surface of the water, the new-found breeze cooling your head. After fully inflating, take your last deep breath from your regulator and as you slowly exhale, switch to your snorkel. Watch how you effortlessly snorkel back into shore, with the waves now assisting you. Observe how you remove your fins when you reach knee-deep water and then carefully climb up onto the rocks, then back onto shore. Keep your breath flowing: "inhale 1-2-3-4, exhale 4-3-2-1."

Smile internally, or even externally, as you imagine a calm and effortless dive. Gradually open your eyes. Make some notes in a journal about any thoughts that arose, or observations that occurred to you during your visualization.

Visualization 2: Overcoming a difficulty

If you have been worried about a particular event under water, such as being low on air, you can try visualizing that event happening. Bring some focus to your breath, keep your breathing slow and steady as you visualize the event happening, and visualize yourself remaining calm and solving your problem under water. The more you can visualize yourself facing difficult challenges while remaining calm, the better prepared psychologically you will be for those challenges. We will place this second visualization in the same tropical surroundings as the first one.

Begin by imagining yourself on a boat with your wet suit on, but not quite zipped. As you calmly gather your gear together, express your excitement to your buddy about what you are about to see: this is your first wreck dive and you can't wait. Feel the warm Caribbean Sea breeze in your hair as you zip your wet suit and assemble your gear. As you and your buddy go through your pre-dive safety check, everything seems to be in order. Upon reaching the swim platform, you prepare by taking a calm rhythmic breath: "inhale 1-2-3-4, exhale 4-3-2-1."

Witness how you secure your mask and regulator to your face and your other gear to your torso, and how you and your buddy complete simple giant strides off the boat. You can take a bird's eye view as you watch yourself signal to the boat that you are okay after establishing buoyancy, and as you snorkel to the line. See you and your buddy reach the mooring buoy and look down to see the wreck, a huge boat sitting at 80 feet, visible through the clear turquoise water. Notice the dive boat gently bobbing as you take your bearings. Smell the salt of the sea. Keep your breath flowing: "inhale 1-2-3-4, exhale 4-3-2-1."

After making your checks and noting the time, follow your descent. Feel the roughness of the rope against your palm as you grip the line to steady yourself. Visualize the color changes and feel the temperature changes as you break through the first few feet. Feel your ears release as you equalize and slowly make your way down the line. You can even physically smile as you face your buddy. Keep your breath flowing: "inhale 1-2-3-4, exhale 4-3-2-1."

Find yourself coming to the ship's upper decks and view the artificial reef that it has created. As you prepare to enter the ship, see yourself tense up a bit, wondering if you want to take the route the divemaster laid through the ship with his line. Sense your body tense as you question whether the visibility will be good enough to navigate your way through the ship if you lose the line. Feel your breath speed up and your heart race as you get a bit anxious, but then witness how you remind yourself to pause and take some deep breaths to calm down: "inhale 1-2-3-4, exhale 4-3-2-1."

See your buddy signal to ask if you are okay. See yourself signal back affirmatively. As you penetrate the wreck, notice the darkness surrounding you. Feel your legs move with the frog style of finning to avoid kicking up silt. You lead the way through the wreck, the line sliding along your hand, and your buddy following you. Watch yourself use smooth, steady strokes, originating each stroke from your hip and maintaining a neutral torso. Observe the hard metal edges of the ship now obscured by various coral formations. Keep your breath flowing: "inhale 1-2-3-4, exhale 4-3-2-1."

Watch your movements through the various compartments and decks on the ship. Like an outside observer watching a film, watch your brain wonder what life must have been like aboard this freighter and how people could have slept in such cramped quarters. Feel yourself control your buoyancy by using subtle muscle contractions and the pacing of your breath. Check out your surroundings with deep curiosity as you enter the galley and imagine what they must have used for ingredients. Keep your breath flowing: "inhale 1-2-3-4, exhale 4-3-2-1."

Suddenly you feel your breath restrained, like breathing through a straw. Finally it occurs to you to look at your air gauge and you realize you have only 100 PSI left in your tank. View your watch and realize that only 20 minutes have elapsed, and that your buoyancy control has been great, so you realize you must have had a leak. Feel yourself agitated at the faulty rental equipment and feel yourself anxious about being out of air at 80 feet. Watch yourself calm down as you remember the number one thing you need to do is to steady your breath: "inhale 1-2-3-4, exhale 4-3-2-1."

Find yourself spinning around to get your buddy, only to discover he has disappeared. Watch yourself again panic and curse him for not staying close to you. But then you accept your responsibility as well for being too excited about the wreck to check back with your buddy frequently. Notice your body release the tension and slow down as you again resume the steady pace of your breath: "inhale 1-2-3-4, exhale 4-3-2-1."

With a clear and rational mind, you decide to get your buddy's attention by circling your dive light into the rooms behind you. Instead of racing around the ship, you decide to stay put and signal. You reason that you will wait for your buddy until you have only 20 PSI remaining and then exit the wreck through the large hole nearby to do a controlled emergency swimming ascent. Even though you can feel your air reserve diminishing, you still keep your breath flowing steady: "inhale 1-2-3-4, exhale 4-3-2-1."

View your buddy now swimming towards you, responding to the signal of your light. Watch how you calmly but firmly signal to him that you are out of air and that you need his octopus. Feel the security as he grabs your BCD to make sure you stay connected. Feel yourself take one last deep breath from your regulator and feel how you blow small air bubbles as you purge your buddy's octopus and put it in your mouth. Notice how your composure strengthens as you return to your breath pattern: "inhale 1-2-3-4, exhale 4-3-2-1."

Observe you and your buddy slowly and carefully exit the ship and begin an immediate ascent, away from the mooring line. Feel yourself connected, safe and calm as you slowly ascend and patiently make a safety stop. Finally feel yourself breaking through the surface of the water and the breeze stirring your wet hair. Because your leaky regulator drained your tank, you have to orally inflate your BCD, but find security in having your buddy there to keep you afloat as you do so. Watch how you and your buddy snorkel back to the boat, now a much longer swim because you ascended away from the line, but find yourself taking your time, using long smooth fin strokes. Observe how you reach the boat and remove your fins, passing them to one of the boat mates. Feel your grateful climb up the swim ladder. Reflect on how calm you stayed during this challenge and find gratitude for your training and mental preparation. Keep your breath flowing: "inhale 1-2-3-4, exhale 4-3-2-1."

You can of course demand a new regulator from the dive operator, but for a few moments, reflect on your success. You handled a difficult and serious challenge with a clear and calm mind. Remind yourself that on future wreck dives you and your buddy will perform a bubble-check at 20 feet, checking your gear for leaks, to minimize the risk of this situation repeating itself.

Gradually open your eyes. Make some notes in a journal about any thoughts that arose, or observations that occurred to you during your visualization.

Create your own visualization practice

After practicing with these visualizations once or twice, you will undoubtedly create your own. Some people prefer audible cues during visualization, so you could even write a script and record it onto a CD. We suggest having a friend speak the script, because most people find the sound of their own voice distracting.

You can play some music during visualization if that helps, but avoid anything with lyrics, or too many tempo or volume changes, because that can be distracting. To prepare for your visualization exercise, you can spend a few minutes looking at some underwater photographs first. This can help your mind form clearer pictures as you work through your exercise.

Many thoughts and ideas will surface during a visualization practice, so start keeping some logs every time, and notice if your thoughts change over the course of a few months as both your yoga and diving experiences change.

Meditation practice

Meditation is slightly different from visualization and can take many forms. In visualization, the brain is focused, whereas in meditation, we let the brain relax. Often you will hear people say, "Just clear your mind," which is technically impossible because your brain is constantly sending and receiving signals to and from the rest of your body. Instead of clearing your mind, a better way to think about meditation is simply quieting your active mind, which means slowing down your thoughts. There are guided meditations or mantra-based meditations where you chant the same phrase over and over. A very basic form of meditation is just silently observing your breath.

When you practice Corpse, you are practicing meditation. The important component of meditation is stillness. We don't allow much time for stillness in our society. Sure, we have lots of lethargy and couch-sitting, but that is different from stillness. Stillness means turning off the television. Just taking a few minutes for a time-out every day can help you better cope with the rest of your day. When you travel with a group—especially on a dive boat where there's not a lot of space—this practice is essential. Allowing yourself a few minutes of internal focus and stillness recharges the battery bank of your mind. You don't need a special set up for meditation; in fact, staring at the horizon for 10 minutes while practicing deep breathing and simply allowing yourself to just be can work wonders.

In fact, scuba diving can be a form of meditation. When you dive and use rhythmic breathing, you change to a more relaxed state. Divers take the role of an observer—hopefully you are not actively trying to change the behavior of aquatic life, but instead are just observing it. While diving, allow your thoughts stay with the present movement, becoming almost one with your surroundings, and try not to get caught up in over-analysis or worry. By practicing meditation on land, you can work towards achieving a more meditative state in the water, which will make diving an even more enjoyable activity for you.

You can try meditating right before entering the water by staring at the horizon and using the same slow, deep, rhythmic breathing pattern. So, a few minutes of deep breathing before you enter the water is a great way to de-stress before a dive. Also, at the end of your dives, give yourself a few moments to let your brain reflect upon all the sensory input you just received.

You must be the change you want to see in the world.

—Mahatma Gandhi

Yoga philosophy and application to diving

So far we have only briefly mentioned the different limbs of royal yoga. In this section we provide an overview of all eight limbs, so that you have a clearer picture of this practice. There are numerous texts out there that describe these limbs in detail, but we wanted to give you a basic primer on them, so you can draw some connection between the physical practice and the psychological practice of yoga.

Instead of thinking of these limbs as an eight-step program, you can think of them as a continuum, or rather as various aspects of yoga that can happen simultaneously as you practice. If you want to study more yoga philosophy, pick up a translation of *The Yoga Sutras of Patanjali*; you will want a book with in-depth commentary, as the *sutras*, or "threads of wisdom," are quite terse.

In order, here are the eight limbs of royal yoga:

1. *Yamas:* These are restraints, or things we should not do in our day-to-day life.

2. *Niyamas:* These are actions (literally, "not inactions"), or things we should do in our day-to-day life.

3. *Asana:* This tells us to find a comfortable seat, but yoga practitioners consider all kinds of odd positions to be comfortable seats, giving us the various yoga poses.

4. *Pranayama:* Technically this means mastery of life force, but we generally take to mean practicing various breathing exercises to regulate the flow of oxygen in the body.

5. *Pratyahara:* This means withdrawal from the senses, which means bringing your focus inward, and not staying vigilant of the sights, sounds, smells, tastes and sensations around you.

6. *Dharana:* You can interpret this as concentration and focus, such as the concentration you use during the visualization practice.

7. *Dhyana:* This means meditation, or the absence of distracting thoughts. The path to meditation usually leads first through withdrawal from the senses, then through concentration.

8. *Samadhi:* This is a state of unadulterated and unqualified bliss. Many people say that you do the work of yoga to attain this bliss; however, we see it as more as brief blissful moments in time, and hopefully you can find more of those moments and learn to extend them. We believe scuba divers can experience this bliss, once they have become at one with the aquatic world surrounding them.

The first two limbs deal with lifestyle and behavior, which makes them very accessible to us. There are five restraints and five actions within those two limbs that serve as lifestyle guidelines. What follows is our interpretations of those restraints and actions in terms of how they can shape your approach to diving.

As you read these, keep the word 'moderation' in the back of your mind. Yoga literature describes it as following the middle path—between the extremes—which is an excellent way to view these guidelines.

Yogis also believe that the teacher inside your own mind is the best teacher around, and that if you stop and listen to your own internal wisdom, you will learn a great deal. We hope that you spend some time thinking about what these restraints and actions mean to you, and that they help you refine your own moral code.

Restraints *(Yamas)*

There are five restraints that serve as lifestyle guidelines. We have restricted our discussions of these guidelines to the realm of diving, but you can find a plethora of discussion in books, magazines and Web forums on applying these to other areas of your life.

Non-violence *(Ahimsa)*

Non-violence means not causing or allowing harm. It means treating yourself with respect, preventing others from being harmed, and not damaging the people and the world around you. Honoring your personal limits as a diver, being an attentive dive buddy, and not disturbing aquatic life during your dives are three simple ways to apply this restraint to diving.

We encourage you to push yourself beyond these simple acts, though. For example, another way to prevent the abuse of aquatic life is to encourage sustainable fishing methods. (We do not interpret the restraint of non-violence to mean that you must be a vegetarian.) Drift net fishing and bottom trawling both cause tremendous damage in our oceans, destroying the abundant life we want to enjoy during our dives. Some farmed seafood are raised in polluted water from overcrowded ponds, which requires unsafe levels of fungicides or antibiotics to prevent the farmed life from dying. These methods of supplying seafood to consumers represent extreme ends of the fishing industry that cause harm. If you decide to eat seafood, you can follow a reasonable middle path by verifying that the seafood comes from responsible vendors. Or, you can responsibly harvest the seafood yourself. This might cost you some extra money and time, but it's a worthwhile price to help preserve the aquatic life that makes your dive vacations memorable.

Truthfulness *(Satya)*

When it comes to diving, honesty is a life-saving policy. Diving within your limits means being honest with dive operators about your training, and being honest with yourself about whether you feel up to the dive that day.

To promote truthfulness, we implement a policy where anyone can call off a dive for any reason, without having to justify it. We encourage you to do the same with your dive buddies; it's a policy that saves lives.

Non-stealing *(Asteya)*

Non-stealing means just that: don't steal. Divers love discovering treasure, but when you take something from a dive site, you take something away from everyone who will dive that site after you. You can view it this way: you started your dive without that trinket, so by leaving it on the bottom you are not losing anything—you are simply ending the dive with as much stuff as you started. Or, imagine if everyone who dove a wreck took a piece of it with them, there would be no more wreck to dive. With the advances in underwater electronics, you no longer need to take artifacts to prove you made a challenging dive; instead, you can take great photographs or video, preserving the site and its artifacts for everyone who follows.

Continence *(Brahmacharya)*

This restraint calls for control of your bodily functions in order to maintain vigor. We temper this restraint with the concept of moderation, or the middle path, which guides all interpretations of yoga. For example, one margarita after a day of diving may refresh you, while five margaritas after a day of diving will sap your energy and generally make you unfit to dive the next day. Physically challenging dives are fun, but when you find yourself exhausted after your second dive, you should sit out the third of the day. We always want to have enough energy to feel confident when we dive, and this restraint teaches us to know when we have reached our limits. It sounds rather unoriginal, but moderation in all things is the best guideline for a healthy, vigorous life.

Non-greed (Aparigraha)

Practicing non-greed means not being greedy about your dive. This means operating in a spirit of collaboration rather than competition. Instead of competing to see who can come up with the most amount of air, for example, work together to learn different buoyancy and relaxation techniques from one another. When you view your dive buddies as team members—people who can help you improve your own abilities and friends you want to help succeed as well—diving becomes a more enjoyable collaborative experience for everyone.

Actions (Niyamas)

In addition to the five restraints, there are five actions. Some people equate the restraints and actions with the Ten Commandments, but they are not so set in stone. Think of them more as ten golden rules, and remember that it's your job to give each of these some thought, and interpret them for yourself.

Some of the actions have a spiritual tone. However, practicing yoga is not adopting a new religion; it is a physical and mental discipline—one that helps you align day-to-day life with your spiritual beliefs, whatever they may be.

Purity (Saucha)

This action teaches us proper hygiene. Purity informs us to take excellent care of our bodies and our physical environment. By keeping your body and your gear clean and healthy, you will have far fewer problems. If you keep yourself in good physical condition, the physical aspects of diving will come more easily to you, allowing you to better enjoy the experience. If you know that you have maintained your gear properly, you won't be troubled about your gear and you will be more able relax and enjoy your dive.

Finally, remember that purity is tempered by moderation. You want to keep your body, mind, and environment clean without becoming obsessive.

Contentment *(Samtosha)*

Contentment means being happy where you are right here right now. This means learning to enjoy your diving, regardless of whether it lived up to your expectations. When you dive, focus on the things you did see, rather than the things you did not see. If some people on your trip saw a shark, but you saw mainly angelfish instead, try to enjoy your experiences, rather than feel disappointed at what you feel you missed.

Note that contentment does not mean that you stop learning and improving your skills. Instead, it teaches you to be happy where you are; with each new challenge, pause to celebrate all that you have accomplished.

Commitment *(Tapas)*

Tapas translates to the word 'fire' and we think of it as the fire in our belly that drives us to achieve. We use commitment to complete our training courses, despite gear mishaps or even our own anxiety. Commitment also helps us adhere to our core principles, and gives us the courage to act in accordance with what we believe.

Of course, contentment balances commitment because it teaches you to be happy along the way, and not use the phrases "if only" or "when I become" to speak of happiness as a future state. Truthfulness also balances commitment because it teaches you to be honest when you cannot finish something. You might commit to doing three dives in one day, but if you find yourself exhausted after the second dive, you realize that your primary commitment is to your own safety and to the safety of your buddy, so you refrain from the third dive, despite your initial commitment to make three dives.

You can use a yoga pose practice as an exercise in commitment. Decide that for two weeks you will practice a few rounds of the Sun Salutation every morning and then stick to it. However, if you strain your muscles and the Sun Salutation becomes painful, recognize that you have committed as much as is reasonable, and allow your body to rest. You can return to your commitment after you have healed.

Spiritual study (*Svadyaya*)

We interpret this action as taking time to study whatever it is that awakens your spirit. Diving awakens our spirit by giving us an opportunity to interact with a world that is omnipresent yet hidden from most people. For divers, spiritual study can mean learning more about the aquatic life we encounter on our dives, and developing a profound respect for the intricacies of underwater ecosystems.

Since an overarching principle of yoga is that you are ultimately your own best teacher, spiritual study also teaches you to spend time reflecting on what you have learned. By keeping detailed dive logs—where you discuss your thoughts, your ideas, and any personal discoveries that you made during your dives—you can more easily reflect on what you have learned from your previous dives.

Surrender to the divine *(Ishvar Pranidhanam)*

You can interpret surrender to the divine as devoting your life to your beliefs. As divers, we see it as practicing a reverence for the oceans and treating our waters and their inhabitants with sincere respect. We see the divine during every dive, in the natural beauty that surrounds us.

Surrendering also helps us realize that we cannot control everything. Even the most carefully planned dive trip can go awry when an unexpected storm moves in. By accepting our lack of total control, we learn to practice contentment when a thunderstorm means we play board games instead of diving that day.

The Sanskrit character **OM**, which represents the sound of the universe.

Happiness comes when your work and words are of benefit to yourself and others.

—Buddha

Go practice

We hope you have enjoyed our discussion on yoga for scuba divers and hope this gives you a good baseline to begin. We encourage you to practice the poses in this book and to seek out a yoga class in your area and attend regularly. There are numerous styles of yoga out there and you should try a few different styles until you find the teacher, the timeslot and the style that work best for you. This is a personal choice. If you are a beginner, take a beginner class, because styles can vary and you want to learn the basics of a style first. If there are no classes convenient in your area, you can try some yoga videos for a home practice.

In this book we have used some *Vinyasa* yoga, which means flowing from pose to pose with the breath. *Hatha* yoga is an umbrella term for many styles, including *Vinyasa,* but there are many teachers who label their classes simply *Hatha* yoga. *Hatha* fuses the words for sun and moon in Sanskrit and it essentially means balancing aggressive sun energy with receptive moon energy. In your physical pose practice, you do this by doing more strengthening poses, such as Plank, along with more relaxing poses, such as Lying Spinal Twist.

While we love the fact that yoga requires no gear, we realize that many scuba divers are gear junkies, so here's our quick list of helpful yoga gear. A sticky mat is useful to prevent sliding around and for providing extra cushion for kneeling poses. A strap is great when you need extra extension to reach your feet or your hands in certain poses, but you can use an old necktie, sock or a small towel as a strap. For the visualization exercises or meditation, sitting on a pillow cross-legged with your knees on the floor is great, since it helps your spine stay long. Of course, you could also practice meditation seated in a chair as well.

In addition to learning more about yoga, we hope you continue your diving education as well. Besides taking classes that improve your buoyancy control and technical abilities, you should take some classes that help you better understand the natural world of our oceans. The more you learn, the more you grow.

The search for truth is more precious than its possession.

—Albert Einstein

Resources

The following resources may help you develop your own practice. There are numerous resources on yoga out there, but here's a quick list to get your started.

Books

Anatomy of Hatha Yoga: A Manual for Students, Teachers, and Practitioners by H. David Coulter

The Yoga Sutras of Patanjali translation and commentary by Sri Swami Satchidananda

DVDs

A.M. and P.M. Yoga for Beginners starring Rodney Yee, Patricia Walden, and Steve Adams

Freeing the Bird of Prana starring Tias Little

The Pleasure of Strength starring Ana Forrest

Web sites

8th Element Diving: www.8thElementDiving.com

8th Element Yoga: www.8thElementYoga.com

DAN Divers Alert Network: www.DiversAlertNetwork.org

Project Aware: www.ProjectAware.org

Punk Rock Yoga: www.PunkRockYoga.com

Yoga Basics: www.YogaBasics.com

Yoga Journal Pose Library: www.YogaJournal.com/poses/

Being loved by someone gives you strength, while loving someone deeply gives you courage.

—Lao Tzu

About the authors

Kimberlee Jensen Stedl is a certified yoga instructor (200-hour Registered Yoga Teacher with the Yoga Alliance). She is certified in the YogaFit® style, and has experience in a variety of yoga disciplines including Iyengar, Viniyoga and Kundalini, having practiced since 1997. Kimberlee founded Punk Rock Yoga®, an international yoga movement, in 2003.  Kimberlee is a member of the American Council on Exercise (ACE) Continuing Education Faculty and has been an ACE Certified Group Fitness Instructor since 1992. She loves warm-water diving and is an advanced open water diver who plans to become a divemaster in 2008. Kimberlee established 8th Element Yoga (www.8thElementYoga.com) to support her diverse yoga interests. Kimberlee has a bachelor's degree in Journalism.

Todd Stedl is an Open Water Scuba Instructor certified through the Professional Association of Diving Instructors (PADI). He has been a dive professional since 2002, assisting as a divemaster for numerous instructors before becoming an instructor himself and establishing 8th Element Diving (www.8thElementDiving.com). Todd is an avid Puget Sound diver who enjoys tropical diving and is now discovering the world of alpine lake and river diving. He is also a regular yoga practitioner and was surprised to discover how much practicing yoga improved his scuba diving. Todd holds a doctorate in chemistry from the University of Washington and has been a professional writer since 2000.

Together, Kimberlee and Todd have led workshops in the Seattle area that teach yoga for scuba divers. This *Yoga for Scuba Divers* book represents the fusion of their passions and their knowledge. And yes, they are happily married as well.

For questions, or to invite Todd and Kimberlee to present a workshop or retreat, contact Kimberlee at DoYoga@8thElementYoga.com or Todd at GoDive@8thElementDiving.com.

Printed in the United States
206879BV00001B/199/A

9 780615 154329